PRAISE FOR

Henri Nouwen and Soul Care

A MINISTRY OF INTEGRATION

"In this helpful contribution to the growing body of literature assessing the life and ministry of Henri Nouwen, Wil Hernandez examines the multiple dimensions of ministry Henri embodied with such authenticity and effectiveness. Focusing especially on Henri's legendary gift of soul care to thousands, the author lifts up Nouwen's singular genius for integrating spirituality with psychology, ministry, and theology."
    —*Marjorie J. Thompson, author of* Soul Feast, *and architect of the* Companions in Christ *resource series for small-group spiritual formation*

"Henri Nouwen, the beloved companion, friend, guide, mentor, and spiritual director, modeled a humble, human ministry that offered drink from a very deep well. Wil Hernandez is mapping a path to that wellspring. Understanding that spirituality is to religion as justice is to law, Nouwen spoke to a world of *incoherent* spirituality with a voice for *coinherence,* teaching the balance and rhythm of the three spiritual movements—inward, outward, and upward (toward self, others, and God)—and uniting them with parallels, paradox, and moments of surprising epiphany. The author offers us [this] second book on Nouwen that explores his understanding and practice of ministry as an integrative art of service that unites multiple disciplines in the care of souls. This is a book for spiritual directors and directees, for ministers and lay spiritual guides, a book to be savored and shared with others."
    —*Dr. David Augsburger, professor of pastoral care, Fuller Theological Seminary, and author of* Dissident Discipleship

"Wil Hernandez masterfully unfolds the complexity, spiritual depth, and richness of Henri Nouwen's genuinely held beliefs about the intersection of spirituality and ministry. He takes us on an intentional journey through the movements of grace that brought Nouwen to his own spiritual and ministerial integration. This book challenges us to visit our own story as we strive to grapple with the challenges of ministry. Wil truly speaks to the heart of the matter."

—*Sr. MaryAnne Huepper, CSJ, executive director,*
Center for Spiritual Development, Orange, California

"While Wil Hernandez's first book probed the shape and depth of Nouwen's integrative spirituality, this companion work shows how Nouwen nurtured spirituality in others. Wil roots Nouwen's ministry within the best literature on spiritual friendship, guidance, mentoring, and spiritual direction—each a distinct kind of spiritual influence. He shows how Nouwen's approach cannot be reduced to any one of these but was integrative of them all. Wil has given us a significant piece of writing that enlarges our understanding of how Nouwen carried out his ministry of spiritual transformation in the lives of others."

—*L. Paul Jensen, PhD, executive director,*
The Leadership Institute, California

"The brilliance of Nouwen has always been his journey into the beauty and complexity of the human soul and the unpacking of its relationship to God. Dr. Hernandez explores the wealth of his insights, bringing clarity and substance to our own life journey."
—*Keith J. Matthews, DMin, Professor of Spiritual Formation*
and Contemporary Culture, Haggard Graduate School
of Theology, Azusa Pacific University

"Wil Hernandez understands Henri Nouwen—as a person, a friend, a guide, a mentor, and a director. This book is his gift to us, so that Henri can companion us as we too engage in our transformational journey and experience 'Christ in us, the hope of glory.'"
—*Karl Bruce, director, Spiritual Formation Alliance Network*

"Wil Hernandez has effectively used the category of *soul care* to offer us another window into the heart of the late Henri Nouwen. Nouwen's journey as a pastor of souls embodied and enlivened so many of the concepts he reflected on and wrote about. Wil has brought these many pieces together to help us understand the ways Nouwen remained ever-interested in and so often helpful to people in their processes of spiritual growth. In so doing, the author calls on the story of Nouwen's journey to help us ask the right questions about how to be spiritual friends, guides, pastors, and above all, companions to each other."
—*Bob Hurteau, PhD, director, Center for Religion and Spirituality, Loyola Marymount University*

"In this practical and illuminating book, Wil Hernandez brings a clear, fresh lens to the infinitely engaging life and work of Henri Nouwen. We are given glimpses into his ministry of soul care as it manifested through friendship, mentoring, direction, teaching, writing, and his generous public revelation of his heart and life. We finish the book encouraged in our own practices of soul care, directed to notice common temptations and their antidotes, and, ultimately, reminded of the One who sustains our lives and ministries."
—*Susan S. Phillips, PhD, executive director, New College Berkeley, Graduate Theological Union, and author of* Candlelight: Illuminating the Art of Spiritual Direction

"At a time when the church is recognizing anew the deep need for spiritual transformation and for proven guides to come to its aid, Wil Hernandez brings us the tested wisdom of Henri Nouwen. The reader will be grateful for Hernandez's mining of Nouwen's deep insights into the multifaceted ministry of soul companioning. Whether you are a vocational spiritual leader or anyone hungry to grow in responsiveness to God, you'll benefit from this book."
—*Alan Fadling, spiritual director and coordinator of the Journey Retreats*

Henri Nouwen
and Soul Care

Henri Nouwen and Soul Care

A MINISTRY OF INTEGRATION

Wil Hernandez

PAULIST PRESS
New York/Mahwah, N.J.

Cover photograph by Ron van den Bosch Productions
Cover design by Joel Dasalla
Interior artwork by Jason Chen. Used with permission.
Book design by Lynn Else

Library of Congress Cataloging-in-Publication Data

Hernandez, Wil.
    Henri Nouwen and soul care : a ministry of integration / Wil Hernandez.
        p. cm.
    Includes bibliographical references (p.   ) and index.
    ISBN-13: 978-0-8091-4546-1 (alk. paper)
    1. Nouwen, Henri J. M. 2. Spiritual formation. 3. Church work. I. Title.
    BX4705.N87H47 2008
    282.092—dc22

                                                                2008018462

Published by Paulist Press
997 Macarthur Boulevard
Mahwah, New Jersey 07430

www.paulistpress.com

Printed and bound in the
United States of America

Contents

Foreword

In his letter more than a year prior to his becoming our permanent pastor, Henri Nouwen asked only that we provide him a quiet place for ten days in the Daybreak community where he could be alone to write. He arrived, settled into a routine, and faithfully worked each day until mid-afternoon, when his extroverted personality sent him scrambling for casual relationships with community members.

After only a few days, Raymond, a member of the community with a disability, suffered a serious accident and was hovering between life and death in intensive care. Angry because of Daybreak's lack of proper supervision, the family forbade community members to visit Raymond at the hospital. Upon hearing this news, Henri borrowed a car and was met by Raymond's father in the waiting room connected to intensive care.

"I am a priest," Henri said, "and I'm here to be with you and with Raymond. Tell me what is happening for your son and for you." While Henri listened attentively, Raymond's father grieved his son's condition and expressed helplessness in the face of it. In time Henri asked, "Have you blessed your son?"

Confused by the question, Raymond's dad replied, "No. Why? I don't understand what you are talking about. And I wouldn't even know where to begin."

Henri answered, "This is important. Come, I will help you. A father must bless his son. If Raymond dies, he will make that passage under your blessing, and if he lives, he will live with the blessing of his father. This is a very special thing to do. You will find stories of how fathers blessed their sons all through the Hebrew Scriptures."

At the bedside in intensive care, Henri prompted the weeping parent to put his hands on Raymond and to whisper into his ear all the ways in which he loved his son. Then Henri invited him to announce to Raymond all the precious gifts that he had brought to their family. Finally, Henri said, "Tell Raymond how you are feeling right now, what you want for him, and encourage him to choose to live."

Wiping the tears from his eyes in the waiting room afterward, the father asked Henri, "Who are you? And who sent you here?" Henri explained that he was visiting L'Arche Daybreak. He went on to say how the community members were suffering because of what happened to Raymond and were awaiting news of Raymond's condition. When Henri was leaving, he promised to return the following day. The father's parting words were, "Please ask the people of Daybreak to come with you. We want them to visit Raymond."

Back in the community of Daybreak, Henri set about pastoring us to support Raymond in the only way we could: spiritually. Henri wanted each of the eight homes to have a picture of Raymond for the dinner table. One by one, Henri visited every home to share about his visit to Raymond and to answer the many questions of community members about life and death. Finally he explained, after the evening meal, how each one could pray for Raymond and for his family.

"Speak," he told us, "and tell our merciful God how you feel about Raymond. Ask for Raymond's healing. And then tell Our Lord to stay with Raymond if he lives or if he dies."

Henri told us to talk together about Raymond, to tell stories, to laugh and to weep together, assuring us that our thoughts, words, and heartfelt prayer would support Raymond at a time when he was so powerless in our midst.

Henri's presence during this "writing visit" was remarkably supportive, helping us through a very difficult time. At the end of ten days and following many visits to the hospital, Henri took his leave. Raymond was on the road to recovery, and community members were reconciled with Raymond's family.

This story illustrates the multidimensional and multidisciplinary nature of Henri Nouwen's ministry, as ably tackled by Wil Hernandez in *Henri Nouwen and Soul Care: A Ministry of Integration*. Wil unpacks the broad spectrum of roles exemplified by Henri. Not only are there descriptions of words like *pastor, priest, mentor, counselor, friend, guide,* and *bridge-builder,* but Wil also provides living examples and testimonies from those who encountered Henri in these various roles in their lives.

Henri Nouwen and Soul Care: A Ministry of Integration points every Christian to the benefits of choosing to be guided by a spiritual director on the spiritual path. As readers we are able to identify with those who brought their important questions to Henri, and, because of these many examples and connections, to realize that it is possible for all spiritual seekers to learn this discipline. But the book doesn't stop at helping us to be mentored. The author awakens confidence in us to reach beyond ourselves and become spiritual friends with others close to us. We are taught what it means to mentor another. In chapter 3 we read:

> The mentor's standard question to the mentoree is basically "How can I help you get to where you are going?" This is exactly the kind of question Henri Nouwen would ask the individuals to whom he ministered. His aim was always that people might be freed to be who they were called to be. Herein lies the heart of a real mentor, one of selfless giving for the other's sake.

The author is not telling us we have to know the answers to all of life's questions. He is helping us to listen deeply and to trust that the answers lie within the other. The role of the spiritual friendship is to encourage and free one another to trust our own deep, spiritual integrity.

Wil generously shares essential gems of spiritual wisdom gleaned from his studies of Henri as priest, pastor, and prophet. He makes a balanced presentation of Henri's human vulnerability and spiritual power, using an amazing blend of psychology and spirituality. Without going overboard, Wil announces how all these elements work together in Henri, in the spiritual seeker, and in the minister.

Henri is portrayed in this volume, a companion to Wil's *Henri Nouwen: A Spirituality of Imperfection,* as one of the most effective care-providers of all time. Wil captures the essence of Henri's ministry in chapter 4 when he says,

Henri Nouwen was a man for others. He gave unreservedly of himself because he had a full self to give, a self anchored upon his true, spiritual identity before God as God's beloved (*BJ*:June 3). Therefore, Nouwen could minister as one who "had the authority of clarity, vulnerability, and truth...[and] was able to do what Jesus did—to take the smallest encounters, the simplest experiences, and the most common human flaws, and cast them in a light which revealed them as vehicles for the grace of God."

It isn't often that we find a scholarly work that is likewise pastoral. And it isn't every day that such concentrated considerations around soul care call us to a deeper inner journey and to a more conscious walk together as members of the human family.

By sharing such thoughtful selections from the fruits of his research, Wil unwittingly becomes *our* mentor. His explanations and his analyses convey a spirit of soul care and nurture, as well as the characteristics of spiritual companioning. Like Henri, Wil Hernandez is an impassioned spiritual companion and guide.

Sr. Sue Mosteller, CSJ
Literary Executrix of the Henri Nouwen Legacy

Preface

On September 21, 2006, the initial printed copies of my first book, *Henri Nouwen: A Spirituality of Imperfection,* arrived at the warehouse of Paulist Press—the same date of Henri Nouwen's death a decade earlier. The fact that the release of my book synchronized with the tenth anniversary of Henri Nouwen's death made the work significant for me. All the effort I had put into writing it had paid off.

Apart from teaching a regular course on the spirituality of Henri Nouwen at Fuller Theological Seminary, where the idea of the book was birthed, several other opportunities presented themselves: new courses in other seminaries and universities, workshops and retreats, and numerous speaking engagements in both Catholic and Protestant settings.

At Evergreen Baptist Church, I have had two separate occasions to run an "experimental" six-week series with a couple of selected small groups focusing on Henri Nouwen's spiritual journey. This represented my preliminary attempts to bring Nouwen from the academy, where I first started, to the laypeople in the congregation. The efforts were well worth it. In hindsight, the so-called experiment actually prepared me to embark on the same road beyond my church walls.

One highlight I would like to mention was the first experience I had of conducting a Nouwen workshop for more than four hundred people at the Religious Education Congress hosted annually by the Archdiocese of Los Angeles at the Anaheim Convention Center. This further widened my opportunities to promote Henri Nouwen's spiritual legacy to a more diverse audience of lay and religious folks. The whole experience proved to be so enriching!

The more I am exposed to the wider ecumenical world of Henri Nouwen, the more amazed I am at the immense impact this wounded saint has had, and continues to have. I count it a privilege to be an instrument in propagating his enduring spiritual legacy.

My first book came out of my dissertation work at Fuller Seminary. Initially, I wanted it published ideally as an academic piece. My publisher successfully talked me into making it more readable and accessible to the general public, especially the Nouwen readers. The result is a mildly popular version with a retained textbook feel, allowing me to use it both as a main text for the courses I teach and as a reading reference for the retreat seminars and workshops I now conduct.

Looking back, I have to admit feeling badly about the idea of cutting out large sections of my original dissertation material, including massive content footnotes, appendixes, and one whole chapter dealing with soul care and spiritual formation, which also happened to be the longest chapter. Little did I imagine then that this chapter could well serve as a sequel to my first book.

Here was where I started recognizing the providential hand of God at work. When the Department of Ministry of the Haggard Graduate School of Theology (Azusa Pacific University) in California first offered me an opportunity to teach a summer course on Nouwen, I was told specifically that the course design had to have a strong ministry slant to it. As it turned out, my entire syllabus ended up revolving around Nouwen's integrated approach to soul care and spiritual formation.

Now after two years of teaching from that material, utilizing it, and developing and expanding it to include new resources, it became clear that a sequel to my first book was indeed appropriate. Thus, this present book is a natural progression of the earlier work. If the focus of my first book could be distilled into the conceptual nature of Nouwen's journey and spirituality, that is, its elaborate "contours and textures," this second one could be summed up as representing the "praxis," or the practical and concrete "living out" of such spiritual journey within the context of ministry—in particular, with soul care and spiritual formation as a clear focus.

Henri Nouwen: A Spirituality of Imperfection focused on Nouwen's counterintuitive and countercultural brand of spirituality. It also articulated from Nouwen's perspective the logical relationship of spirituality with psychology, ministry, and theology. The book legitimated how all three of these entities coinhere. In more ways than one, Henri Nouwen's conceptual grasp of their "coinherence" (referring to a "full and mutual sharing of one thing in the complete reality of the other"[1]) serves to function as the interpretive key that unlocks his whole philosophy and practice of ministry. Essentially, this new companion book, *Henri Nouwen and Soul Care,* is about Nouwen's highly integrated form of ministry, which hinges on his equally integrated philosophy of spirituality.

This book is designed primarily to direct the reader's attention to the practical ramifications as well as applications of Henri Nouwen's nuanced understanding of the spiritual journey as it relates to ministry—specifically, soul care and spiritual formation ministry.

My hope is that the reader who is already familiar with my earlier work will find this book to be a worthy sequel—that it will serve not only to complement but also to enhance Nouwen's wealth of insights. This book, in fact, significantly furthers the philosophical framework earlier introduced and translates it into a methodological one, underscoring the practicality of Henri Nouwen's ministry.

A final word about the citation format of this book: for consistency's sake, I am following the format of my first book, using the same parenthetical citation of Henri Nouwen's works within the text (except that in this book, I do not provide an initial full citation of a particular work in the endnotes). The parenthetical citation consists of coded initials of Nouwen's book title followed by page references. For example, (*RO:*12) refers to *Reaching Out: The Three Movements of the Spiritual Life,* page 12.

When citing interviews (personal, phone, or email), I note each of them the first time around (unless, of course, the interview consists of more than one session with the same individual occurring at different dates). This makes more sense, particularly when the direct or indirect quotations are scattered within the same chapter and/or paragraphs. In so doing, the reader is not confronted with repetitive citations in the endnotes.

Acknowledgments

Since much of the material contained in this book came from my original dissertation work, I remain indebted to the folks who assisted me in various capacities early on in this initial project. I wish to make special mention of a few additional people who have significantly contributed to the production of this sequel.

First, I thank Paul MacMahon, the managing editor of Paulist Press, who expressed confidence in me and in the entire project; he persistently saw through to the completion of both the first book and this sequel.

I thank Joel Dasalla, who willingly agreed again to design the cover. Needless to say, this ensured that this book visually retains the same feel as the first one. I also thank Jason Chen for the beautiful pen-and ink-illustration contained in these pages.

Two friends in particular deserve special acknowledgment: Annette Kakimoto of Gardena Valley Baptist Church and Virgil Lew of Evergreen Baptist Church. Without your ever-present support, encouragement, and prayers, I would not have pressed forward with this endeavor.

To all my students in seminary and outside of seminary who have learned and continue to learn together with me about Henri Nouwen and his unique spirituality: you have taught me, sharpened me, and challenged me in ways that you may never realize. Each time I hear you share your own reflections or read your papers, I cannot help but feel an overflow of gratitude for the privilege of taking part in your transforming process through our mutual engagement with Nouwen's works. Through you I am often reminded that there really is a compelling reason why I continue to teach on Henri Nouwen. Thus, I dedicate this new book to all of my students—past and present.

My gratitude also goes to the following people who helped open new doors for me to conduct classes, retreats, and workshops on Henri Nouwen: Sr. MaryAnne Huepper, CSJ, of the Center for Spiritual Development at Orange, California, for inviting me to conduct a six-part study series based on my book; Jan Pedroza for the opportunity to do a Nouwen workshop at the 2008 Religious Education Congress at Anaheim, California; Sr. Julia Costello, DMJ, of Mary & Joseph Retreat Center at Rancho Palos Verdes, California, for offering me to do a one-day retreat/workshop on Nouwen; Dr. Robert Hurteau, for paving the way for me to conduct a weekend class on Nouwen at Loyola Marymount University under the sponsorship of its Center for Religion and Spirituality; Anne Luther of the Institute for Adult Spiritual Renewal (formerly Retreats International), for making it possible for me to teach a weeklong course on Nouwen at Loyola University in Chicago; Cheryl Evanson for including me as a Nouwen retreat facilitator for one of their weekend retreat programs at St. Andrew's Abbey, Valyermo, California; Dr. Mike McNichols of Fuller Southern California, for agreeing to "kick off" the summer course on Nouwen at the same abbey in Valyermo, during that same weekend; Pat Julian of the Franciscan Renewal Center at Scottsdale, Arizona, for hosting the Nouwen retreat I led for my students at Fuller Southwest; Dr. David Timms of Hope International University, California, for opening a summer course track on Nouwen; Colleen Kirkwood, for setting up a Nouwen weekend retreat at Lacey, Washington, for Fuller Northwest students; Dan Wilburn of Lakeland Community Church and Craig Babb of Rhythm of Grace Ministries, for jointly sponsoring a weekend lecture/seminar at Lee's Summit, Missouri; Sr. Evelyn Craig, IHM, and Sheila Blandford, for inviting me to conduct a weekend retreat/seminar at Mount Saint Joseph Conference and Retreat Center at Maple Mount, Kentucky. Thank you all for your interest and enthusiasm to advance the cause of Henri Nouwen's spiritual legacy.

The writing of this book has been a process that I consider part of my communal journey. I've been privileged to be supported by the three communities of which I am proud to belong: The Leadership Institute staff, the Spiritual Formation Alliance Network team (together with the SoCal Spiritual Formation

Partners core group), and the "Sedaqah" core team and "Journey Companions" at Evergreen Baptist Church of Los Angeles. The experience of being with you makes me a firm believer that true community is and can be a reality. I thank God for your being the spiritual companions that you are to me!

I wrote much of this book at various retreat locations within Southern California. I am grateful for the availability of each of these retreat places, which became for me places of "advance" insofar as my focused writing project was concerned: St. Andrew's Benedictine Abbey (Valyermo), Mt. Calvary Monastery and Retreat House (Santa Barbara), Immaculate Heart Community (Santa Barbara), Mary & Joseph Retreat Center (Rancho Palos Verdes), Serra Retreat House (Malibu), Prince of Peace Abbey (Oceanside), Holy Spirit Retreat Center (Encino), and Mater Dolorosa Passionist Retreat Center (Sierra Madre). I appreciate their gracious accommodation and generous hospitality. To me these sacred spaces embody God's gift of solitude and silence.

Henri J. M. Nouwen's Cited Works

(ABBREVIATED TITLE INITIALS IN ALPHABETICAL LIST)

BH   *With Burning Hearts: A Meditation on the Eucharistic Life*

BJ   *Bread for the Journey: A Daybook of Wisdom and Faith*

BM   *Beyond the Mirror: Reflections on Death and Life*

CFM   *A Cry for Mercy: Prayers from the Genesee*

CM   *Creative Ministry*

CR   *Clowning in Rome: Reflections on Solitude, Celibacy, Prayer, and Contemplation*

CYD   *Can You Drink the Cup?*

EM   *Encounters with Merton: Spiritual Reflections*

G!   *¡Gracias! A Latin American Journal*

GD   *The Genesee Diary: Report from a Trappist Monastery*

GG   *Our Greatest Gift: A Meditation on Death and Dying*

HN   *Here and Now: Living in the Spirit*

INJ   *In the Name of Jesus: Reflections on Christian Leadership*

IVL   *The Inner Voice of Love: A Journey Through Anguish to Freedom*

LR   *The Living Reminder: Service and Prayer in Memory of Jesus Christ*

LS   *Lifesigns: Intimacy, Fecundity, and Ecstasy in Christian Perspective*

RD   *The Road to Daybreak: A Spiritual Journey*

RO   *Reaching Out: The Three Movements of the Spiritual Life*

RPS   *The Return of the Prodigal Son: A Story of Homecoming*

SJ   *Sabbatical Journey*

SMW   *Show Me the Way: Readings for Each Day of Lent*

SWC   *The Selfless Way of Christ: Downward Mobility and the Spiritual Life*

WH   *The Wounded Healer: Ministry in Contemporary Society*

WOH   *The Way of the Heart: Desert Spirituality and Contemporary Ministry*

Introduction

Henri Nouwen and the Postmodern Context

As a child of modernity transitioning through the slow but sure passage to postmodernity, Henri Nouwen proved to be ahead of his time as shown by the many ways he anticipated the complex ethos that the advent of postmodernity would introduce. This was not at all uncharacteristic of the way Nouwen normally operated as a person. As John Garvey observes:

> In all of Henri Nouwen's work there is a sense of eagerness, a curiosity, a hunger to see the ways in which the Holy Spirit moves people in our time; and it is not bound either by the sort of traditionalism which fears anything new, on the one hand, or by a slavish concern for the spirit of the age on the other.[1]

Henri Nouwen did exhibit a spirit of openness coupled with a genuinely embracing attitude to life. Perhaps this helps explain how he seemed to nurture an anticipatory perspective, making it so natural for him to envisage whatever might lie ahead.

In reflecting upon his own "history with God," Henri Nouwen revealed some of his most recent realizations just before he passed away. If one were to read between the lines, they contained intriguing insights into some future direction Nouwen apparently was open to exploring:

> During all these years, I learned that Protestants belong as much to the church as Catholics, and that Hindus, Buddhists, and Moslems believe in God as much as Christians do; that pagans can love one another as much as believers can; that the human psyche is multidimensional; that theology, psy-

1

chology, and sociology are intersecting in many places; that women have a real call to ministry; that homosexual people have a unique vocation in the Christian community; that the poor people belong to the heart of the church; and that the spirit of God blows where it wants. All of these discoveries gradually broke down many fences that had given me a safe garden and made me deeply aware that God's covenant with God's people includes everyone. For me personally, it was a time of searching, questioning, and agonizing, a time that was extremely lonely and not without moments of great uncertainty and ambiguity.[2]

Undoubtedly, some of Henri Nouwen's statements (especially the ones with allegedly universalistic undertones) are enough to make conservative Christians nervous. But as his good friend Robert Jonas sensibly remarks, "[Nouwen's] message about Jesus was so clear, powerful, and grounded in the New Testament that they could easily forgive what they considered to be his occasional lapses of judgment."[3]

THE INTEGRATIONIST

Henri Nouwen's deepened, though not necessarily novel, conviction "that the human psyche is multidimensional" and "that theology, psychology, and sociology are intersecting in many places" owed itself to his fundamental integrative leanings. Nouwen's overall conceptual framework concerning integration does sit well with the postmodern penchant for pursuing the ideals of wholeness versus fragmentation. As some observers acknowledge, "Postmodernism, with its valuing of multiple ways of knowing," is, in reality, paving fresh perspectives in this whole integration arena.[4]

Significantly, spirituality has become the "common currency" in the major task of integration. In a way, almost all of Henri Nouwen's writings have preconditioned us to engage in precisely this kind of task. Spirituality, as lived experience, is seen as glue to the integrative thrust. True to postmodern form, the coinherence of spirituality with psychology, ministry, and theology that Henri Nouwen espoused is reckoned by many as a welcome epistemological advance.

THE TRILOGY OF COINHERENCE

Henri Nouwen construed the spiritual life as a threefold movement involving an *inward, outward,* and *upward* thrust—each of which coincides with one's relationship with *self, others,* and *God* (*RO*:13–14). On a one-to-one correspondence, his schema profoundly reflects spirituality's natural correlation with the realms of *psychology, ministry,* and *theology,* which coalesce with each other in dynamic reciprocity.

Therefore, Henri Nouwen's trilogy of coinherence was richly interconnected—psychology and spirituality (knowing *self,* knowing *God*); spirituality and ministry (loving *God,* loving *others*); and theology and spirituality (*knowing* God, *experiencing* God)—the reality of which both his works as well as his experiences more than substantiated. Nouwen's schematic trilogy also ties in directly with the threefold focus of the Great Commandment and defines the nexus of spirituality with psychology (love of self), with ministry (love of neighbor), and with theology (love of God).

THE ENIGMA OF IMPERFECTION

Interestingly, the way Henri Nouwen viewed the spiritual life and its holistic formation projected a postmodern framework. His integrative pursuits, while essentially geared toward coinherence, also accommodated the enigmatic elements of mystery, paradox, and even outright contradictions. In fact, within the context of postmodernity, such emerging realities are now openly celebrated as typifying the "new kind of wisdom."[5]

Anyone familiar with Nouwen's writings can easily detect that he—like Merton, who was fond of dialectics—was at home with antinomies, contradictions, and paradoxes (*EM*:110). He did not just employ them to brilliant effects in many of his writings; Nouwen lived out these same realities. Like John Wesley, who was dubbed "a cluster of paradoxes,"[6] Nouwen lived a paradoxical existence to the hilt, often caught in his own "web of strange paradoxes" (*GD*:14).

Alongside his integrated approach to ministry, Henri Nouwen's personal brand of spirituality, with its trademark of imperfection, connects deeply to a generation that places such a high premium on authenticity, transparency, and a sense of "realness."[7] As a restless seeker, a wounded healer, and a perennial struggler, Nouwen embodied imperfection. The same kind of imperfection is looked upon today as part of postmodern realism—the kind that unabashedly recognizes human finitude, even incorporating certain elements of ambiguity and uncertainty. Ironically in Nouwen, integration and imperfection coexist together. The so-called integrated journey is at the same time an imperfect journey.

To be sure, Henri Nouwen's anticipatory connection with the emerging postmodern ethos can be detected not only through his open embrace of the matrix of paradox and mystery side by side with the counterintuitive mode of imperfection he embodied but likewise through his trilogy of coinherence as the focus of his integrative thrust. Additionally, Henri Nouwen's rhetoric of community—which, as ethicist Elizabeth Bounds rightly qualifies, is "a postmodern discourse"[8]—was foundational to his multifaceted but integrative ministry.

COMMUNITY AND MINISTRY

Henri Nouwen's concept of true spiritual ministry centered on the existential reality of community life. One prominent feature of the postmodern landscape that Nouwen vigorously tackled in his writings is the character of community. Even before the retrieved vocabulary of community began inching its way back into the conversation of our present day, Nouwen already had it covered in several of his works with such depth and breadth of scope. While he did address his own time and specific context, Nouwen plowed deeply enough that his insights still apply to our current situation.

Indeed, many of Nouwen's countercultural emphases continue to challenge our sometimes distorted concepts of community—specifically, spiritual community.[9] Ray Anderson correctly emphasized that "because spiritual formation is closely aligned with the task of being human and existing in the framework of human relationships, the task of spiritual formation is lodged in the intentionality of community."[10] Suffice it to say, Nouwen's communitarian conviction found manifold expressions in the integrated way he conducted his multifaceted ministry of soul care and spiritual formation.

Henri Nouwen's versatile and "multitasking" style of doing ministry holds a special appeal for today's generation, which values integration and multidimensionality in ministry. In all practicality, Nouwen's creative approach—multilevel, multidimensional, multilingual, and multidisciplinary at the same time—goes against the expert-driven, highly individualistic, and overly specialized ministry strategy that is usually one-dimensional, hierarchical, and heavily institutionalized in focus.

Jeff Imbach, the former president of the Henri Nouwen Society in Canada, addressed this same issue by pointing out how Nouwen in fact "challenged a protected institutional approach to ministry" and advocated instead a posture of "solidarity with others rather than in authority over them." At the same time, Jeff was quick to add that while Nouwen anticipated one of the themes of postmodernity "in its loss of trust in institutions and hierarchy," he nevertheless infused it "with a deep spirituality that keeps us from throwing out the baby with the bathwater so to speak."[11] Henri Nouwen did utilize good balance and integration between what I call a spirituality of ministry and a ministry of spirituality.[12] It is precisely this highly integrated ministry of Henri Nouwen that this book will address.

Chapter Overview

The following four chapters serve to illustrate concretely how Henri Nouwen employed a ministry of integration in his own formational work with people. In effect, these chapters establish the practical expressions of a truly integrated spiritual ministry.

Chapter 1 focuses on the subject of the care and cure of souls and what spiritual nurture generally encompasses. It acquaints the reader with the wide spectrum of soul care ministries under the rubric of spiritual accompaniment, or *companioning*. Specifically, it zeroes in on Nouwen's unique and varied ministry of companionship.

Chapters 2 and 3 highlight the actual ways Nouwen modeled what it is like to be a true spiritual companion—whether it be as a friend, a guide, a mentor, or a director—to others on the journey. These chapters focus more personally on how Nouwen exemplified the integrative ministry of soul care and spiritual formation.

Chapter 4 synthesizes Henri Nouwen's integrated approach to soul care and spiritual formation and summarizes their combined and intersecting dynamics.

The conclusion redirects the final focus back to Henri Nouwen, the minister, who embodied a ministry of integration.

CHAPTER ONE

Spiritual Nurture of the Soul

When we think about the people who have given us hope
and have increased the strength of our soul, we might discover
that they were not the advice givers, warners or moralists,
but the few who were able to articulate in words and actions
the human condition in which we participate and
who encourage us to face the realities of life.
—Henri Nouwen, Reaching Out

It is my belief that Henri Nouwen's holistic mindset became the driving force behind his multifaceted ministry and shaped his methodology into a simultaneously multilingual, multidimensional, and multidisciplinary approach. Henri Nouwen was a minister who functioned more as a generalist than a specialist. When it came to the spiritual nurture of the soul, Nouwen's work automatically combined the dynamics of soul care and spiritual formation into a singular goal.

Soul Care and Spiritual Formation

The fact that the concept of integration—between psychology and spirituality in particular—was ingrained deeply in Henri Nouwen's overall thinking leaves no doubt that he regarded soul care and spiritual formation as one and the same process. Indeed, the formation of both the soul and the spirit springs from a unified goal—wholeness and holiness according to the image of God.

In practice, Nouwen treated soul care and spiritual formation as a holistic endeavor of engaging the disciplines of the mind, heart, and body in order to create space for God.[1] This approach accounts for much of his practical, effective style of ministry—whether it be in his writing, teaching, counseling, mentoring, or giving spiritual guidance or direction. Nouwen was always intent on ministering to the whole person. Never did he attempt to compartmentalize his treatment of individuals. He saw people as made in the image of God and therefore carrying every potential to experience wholeness.

Henri Nouwen does indicate how he conceptually framed as well as integrated the various facets of Christian soul care. Before we discuss soul care any further, it is crucial that we at least have a basic grasp of what we mean when we reference this term *soul*, especially as it pertains to its spiritual nurture.

What Is the Soul?

The concept of the soul is still a riddle as far as our theological and psychological understanding of it is concerned. Space will not permit an exhaustive discussion here of the origin and evolution of such an elusive term. Still, a little background can help explain how we are using the concept here.

Generally speaking, the Christian understanding of the soul has evolved quite considerably from the early Platonic idea of dualism (i.e., body and soul as separate and opposites), to a Cartesian brand of dualism (with its mechanistic emphasis on the mind and body distinction), and on to the neo-Thomistic conception upon which is based the now widely embraced holistic (substance) dualism that underscores the organic unity of the human person (i.e., the unity of body and soul).[2]

It is worth noting that the very origin of the word *psychology* had to do with the study of the human psyche or the soul. Wayne Rollins explains that over time the meaning shifted to the study of the mind, which was regarded as more empirically defensible.[3]

With reference to its evolving history, David Fontana points to a period when "psychology first lost its soul and then its mind" amidst psychological discourse.[4] Surprisingly, by the end of the twentieth century, the concepts of *soul* and *psyche* resurfaced again in both popular and academic contexts.[5] For the most part, both *soul* and *psyche* have historically been understood in reference to "the human person as a center of conscious and unconscious awareness, functioning as an emoting, sensing, perceiving, desiring, imagining, knowing, thinking, willing, dreaming, and developing organism."[6]

Scripture itself is not as crystal clear when it employs the term *soul*. Generally, biblical scholars believe that *soul* refers to one's life and personality.[7] Notwithstanding the attempts of some to offer a concise biblical definition of the soul, theologian Ray Anderson correctly points out that the use of the term *soul* in the Bible seems more functional than "analytical or precise in a philosophical or semantic sense."[8]

The familiar creation account in the Book of Genesis informs us that Adam became a living soul (or a "living being" as the New American Bible renders it) after God breathed life into him. This could explain why Catholic theologian Ronald Rolheiser indicates that the soul represents the principle of energy that animates life as well as the principle of integration that holds our being together and makes us one.[9]

In the traditional Hebrew perception of *nephesh*, the soul "is not something we possess as much as a summing up of our total nature."[10] To put it another way, "humans are beings who are souls rather than bodies that *have* souls."[11] Such delineation places the right focus on the essential unity of personhood—the fact that we are both embodied souls and besouled (or ensouled) bodies.[12]

This statement is not a moot point. Our understanding of spirituality is directly impacted by our understanding of the true nature of the human person. As psychologist James Beck warns, "studying *psyche* in isolation from [the] other terms [heart, mind, will, flesh, body, etc.] is not without hermeneutical risk since these terms often display imbedded and overlapping meanings."[13]

In line with this express unity of personhood, it is therefore appropriate to adopt the use of the term *soul* holistically as the very "essence of a person in his or her wholeness."[14] Psychiatrist-turned-spiritual director Gerald May basically concluded that soul is "who a person most deeply *is*: the essential spiritual nature of a human being."[15] In short, "'soul' signifies the whole person: thoughts, feelings, and movements of the will."[16]

Biblically and theologically, the reality of the soul represents the *self* "as nurtured and sustained in the life of God."[17] As both ontologically substantive in their formation and development, *soul* and *self* can thus be viewed almost synonymously.[18]

The primary identity of the soul, then, as employed in this book is in direct reference to the totality of the person created in the image of God—"a valued, valuing, and valuable being."[19]

Soul Work

Spirituality is not merely about becoming more "divine"—as in absorbing more of God's divine character in us. It is also about becoming more human—or realizing our true personhood and full humanity. This entails the rediscovery of our true self—the original self made in the image of God. Through the interior work of self-confrontation leading to a greater sense of self-awareness, self-discovery becomes an experiential possibility. The process is what ushers one toward wholeness, that focal path toward personal integration that Swiss psychologist Carl Jung believed to be our foremost human drive.

In effect, one cannot speak of the process of spiritual formation without directly associating it with the transformational journey of the self. Employing explicit Christian terms, the spiritual journey has to do with becoming our "true-self-in-Christ."[20] But as writer Sue Monk Kidd reminds us, this involves massive confrontation with our false self in which are ingrained "hardened patterns that we've spent a lifetime creating, patterns that oppose the life of the spirit and obscure our true spiritual identity." Such internal structuring is what Kidd calls soul work— "the deepest meaning of spiritual becoming."[21]

It is thus becoming more apparent that soul work is not some kind of an independent task that is only marginally connected to the spiritual realm. John Calvin's construct of "double knowledge"—referring to the knowledge of the self and the knowledge of God—coincides with the linked idea of the double journey: the soul's inward journey to the self and its upward journey to God.

Just as the knowledge of the self and the knowledge of God inevitably intertwine, so do the inward and the upward journeys. Here is where aspects of the human and the divine likewise intersect—where the experiences of wholeness and holiness come together. Thus it can be said that the soul's journey is itself the spiritual journey and the spiritual journey is really the journey of the soul.

Henri Nouwen obviously sees the interconnectedness between soul work and spiritual work. For one, he believes that solitude, silence, and prayer are the effective paths toward self-knowledge since "they bring us in touch with our sacred center, where God dwells" (*BJ*:March 22). Elsewhere, Nouwen singles out prayer as representing the bridge between the conscious and unconscious dimensions of our lives. According to him, "to pray is to connect these two sides of our lives by going to the place where God dwells." Henri Nouwen therefore concludes that "prayer is 'soul work' because our souls are those sacred centers where all is one and where God is with us in the most intimate way" (*BJ*: January 15).

Care and Cure of Souls

The whole arena of spiritual formation essentially focuses on soul work as a spiritual endeavor. Fundamentally, it pertains to the mysterious inner formation of our spiritual soul. The lifelong process incorporates the elaborate notions of soul renovation, soul shaping, soul becoming, and soul keeping. Concisely put, it is about the care and cure of souls, or soul care in short.

The now familiar and revived notion of soul care finds its historical roots in the ancient concept of the cure of souls that John McNeill chronicled in his classic work *A History of the Cure of Souls*.[22] In his book, McNeill substantiates his case that the cure of souls (as administered by spiritual directors and guides, who were once regarded as physicians of souls [*curatores animarum*]) has been a vast enterprise throughout recorded history among different branches of Christianity.

The Latin phrase *cura animarum* carries the idea of both care and cure. Technically speaking, *cura* in Latin has the primary meaning of "care," with undertones of "cure."[23] This combined idea represents two components that figure centrally in the history of Christian soul care: "the response to the need of a remedy for sin and assistance in spiritual growth"—which, in short, deals with the dual notions of "nurture and support as well as healing and restoration" of souls. Soul care, as it is more popularly understood these days, has as its overarching goal the spiritual formation of the Christian's character.[24] In this connection, soul care and spiritual formation can rightly be viewed along the same strand of helping ministry.

Thomas Oden offers a nuanced picture of soul care within the broad context of pastoral ministry: "Care of souls...means the care of the inner life of persons, the mending and nurturing of this personal center of affect and willing."[25] Another way of stating it is that soul care is really pastoral care.

Henri Nouwen defines care as "the loving attention given to another person" (GG:58). "Care is being with, crying out with, suffering with, feeling with. Care is compassion," as Nouwen further elaborates (*BJ*:February 8). Thus, one cannot separate the idea of care from the practice of compassion since compassion is really the sine qua non of authentic soul care. For Nouwen, "the care of soul is paramount, not the cure of the soul."[26] Nouwen asserts that care is the source of all cure. He goes on to emphasize:

> When care is our first concern, cure can be received as a gift.
> Often we are not able to cure, but we are always able to care.
> To care is to be human. (*BJ*:February 8)

Ray Anderson adds that to stress cure versus care does not only seem presumptuous but can also be dangerous in that ultimately nobody can guarantee cure.[27] Soul care as expressed in spiritual care giving is also far more important and realistic.

The contemporary pastoral theology movement, in which Nouwen became a significant player at one time, reflects efforts to recover and preserve the primary spiritual role of the minister as a soul care provider. Being a pastoral theologian himself, Henri Nouwen maintained the conviction that the care and cure of souls was a spiritual undertaking that ministers ought continually to reclaim for themselves (CM:59). In reality, the ministry of healing originally occupied the primary thrust of the church. Even Carl Jung himself clearly understood that to be the case when he wrote *Modern Man in Search of a Soul* in the late 1930s: "We cannot expect the doctor to have anything to say about the ultimate questions of the soul. It is from the clergyman, not from the doctor, that the sufferer should expect such help."[28] As a matter of fact, for much of the history of the Christian church, ministers have always been looked upon as curates—true physicians of souls.[29]

That said, Tilden Edwards clarifies that the physician of souls is really not an actual healer but that "he or she provides an *environment* for the dominant natural process of healing to take its course."[30] The so-called physician acts more like a midwife, setting the proper context for "the birthing and nourishing of a whole soul." In this regard, we refer to healing generally to mean the process of spiritual care giving aimed at moving people to greater personal integration and wholeness of being.

Healing, Sustaining, Guiding

Indicative of his holistic approach to ministry, Henri Nouwen creatively combined the ministerial tasks of *healing, sustaining,* and *guiding,* which all stand for the same foundational principles of pastoral theology advocated by Seward Hiltner, one of his mentors while at the Menninger Clinic. From Hiltner's perspective, *healing* has to do with the restoration of functional wholeness; *sustaining* involves comforting via upholding or standing by and with a sufferer; *guiding* refers to the shepherding aspect of providing spiritual direction. Hiltner himself plainly viewed healing, sustaining, and guiding as one piece that encompasses the total dimension of shepherding.[31]

Integrating them into his own applied understanding, Henri Nouwen recast these three shepherding functions into the overlapping roles of a *pastor* (one who heals the wounds of the past), a *priest* (one who sustains life in the present), and a *prophet* (one who guides others to the future) (*LR:75*). In his ministry of formation, Nouwen wore all three hats, so to speak, in ways that seemed almost indistinguishable. Different people close to Henri Nouwen saw him through these different shafts of light when it came to the varied ministry roles that he undertook—be it as a pastor, as a priest, or as a prophet.

NOUWEN AS A PASTOR

Sr. Sue Mosteller of the Congregation of Saint Joseph, whose close connection with Henri Nouwen dates back to 1987, perceived Nouwen first and foremost in his role as a pastor. While it is true—as everyone who has worked closely with Nouwen would agree—that his priesthood was in his genes, Sue is convinced that the way he expressed his priesthood was through being a pastor.

Henri Nouwen himself loved that title because that was precisely the role that he felt "called to" at L'Arche Daybreak—the Toronto community where he chose to live for the last decade of his life. Nouwen faithfully pastored this diverse, ecumenical community like a spiritual shepherd, feeding his flock out of the abundance of his own heart.

In Sue's particular case, she felt deeply moved by the manner in which Nouwen broke open God's word, something that never failed to touch her life.[32] Nouwen had a compelling way of allowing the word to come alive in people's hearts. At L'Arche Daybreak, the spiritual lives of the community members were sustained by the spiritual nourishment Nouwen constantly provided in his capacity as its resident pastor—despite his increasingly demanding schedule both within and outside the community.

Even back when he served as professor at Yale University, Henri Nouwen's presence on the faculty was viewed by many (including himself) to be that of a pastor rather than a scholar. It was apparent that "the focus of his interest was, from the beginning, and was to remain, *pastoral*, which is to say people- or person-oriented."[33] Nouwen never once felt apologetic about that.

Ministry for Henri Nouwen was definitely more relation-oriented than content-oriented. He understood his own pastoral function as primarily that of "an articulator of inner events," where, as a result of the skillful use of "pastoral conversation," people can experience "a deep human encounter" leading to self-discovery (*WH*:37, 39). As a pastor, Henri Nouwen proved to be a natural.

NOUWEN AS A PRIEST

To Michael Ford, who composed a written portrait of Henri Nouwen, the image of the priest lingers most in his memory. As he explains it in symbolic terms,

> the Latin word for priest, *pontifex*, means a bridge-builder: the priest is the person who builds a bridge between humanity and God. Through his zest for divine and human communication, Henri paved the way for his readers and friends to experience the presence of God in their lives.[34]

There is a sense in which Nouwen did fulfill this kind of priestly role in both local and universal ways. Through the broad reach of his writing and speaking ministry, the world literally became his parish.

Nouwen's priestly ambition, if one wants to call it that, had its genesis when he was a boy of the very tender age of six and never did he change his mind about it after that (*RPS*:20). Being a priest was central to who he was and the Eucharist defined the spiritual core of his own priesthood. In fact, anyone well-acquainted with Nouwen's writings cannot overlook the glaring reality that his life gravitated around the mystery of the Eucharist (*CR*:79).

Indeed, Henri Nouwen's initial mystical experience occurred very early on in his priestly life, during his postcommunion meditation at his first Mass of Thanksgiving. We do not know exactly what transpired except that Nouwen described that rare moment as "an intimate and mystical experience" (*CYD*:110). Such a private, interior experience, however, found exterior expressions in Nouwen. Directly or indirectly, it impacted how Nouwen effectively utilized the Eucharist as a means to reach out to others inclusively and communally. It is no secret that Nouwen did not have much hesitation practicing open communion in his celebration of the Eucharist, especially when certain situations demanded it.

As a priest, Nouwen always took on the role of a gracious and accommodating spiritual host, freely displaying a spirit of inclusivity. Mary Bastedo, chair of the Spiritual Life Committee at the time Nouwen joined the L'Arche community, made this comment about him: "He lived his priesthood not as something that excluded others but rather as a way to invite others into participation."[35] In every way, Nouwen was a true bridge-builder.

NOUWEN AS A PROPHET

The overall perception of Nouwen was a bit different for Nathan Ball, a close friend of Nouwen's since they first met in 1985 at L'Arche in Troly-Breuil, France. While not discounting Nouwen's pastoral and priestly identities and functions, Nathan viewed Nouwen more in terms of his prophetic role by the way he passionately announced to people a vision for community where people with differences could come together.[36] The diverse community of L'Arche Daybreak is one such materialization of his prophetic voice. In that community Nouwen found a home for himself.

Carolyn Whitney-Brown, who with her family lived in community with Nouwen during the final decade of his life at L'Arche Daybreak, recalled this about him: "Henri continually asked if our life together could be bigger, more generous, more visionary. He didn't want the community to live less than its full prophetic presence in the world."[37] Despite his acknowledged limitations as a person, such as his own woundedness, Nouwen still loomed large in his role as a prophet. Everywhere Nouwen found himself, his natural prophetic bent was unmistakably felt.

Prior to his settling down at L'Arche community, Henri Nouwen proved to be a prophetic voice at Harvard, boldly announcing to all who cared to listen the message of the gospel. Nouwen recognized this as his own vocation. "To speak about Jesus and his divine work of salvation," Nouwen insisted, "shouldn't be a burden or a heavy obligation." Genuinely, he believed that "what we have received is so...rich that we cannot hold it to ourselves but feel compelled to bring it to every human being we meet" (*BJ*:August 6).

With such unswerving commitment, Nouwen did proclaim Jesus rather unashamedly at Harvard—something deemed by many insiders of that institution as a politically incorrect move.

When Nouwen later sensed the constraints of being able to do precisely that on a continual basis, he chose not to compromise what he believed to be his primary calling. He left the Ivy League school without any regret.

By any measure Nouwen was a prophetic agent of change. In her book *Spiritual Guides for Today,* Annice Callahan considers Nouwen as a "prophet of conversion...in the sense of a 'second' conversion," referring to the lifelong process of turning to God.[38] Nouwen was committed to calling people to ongoing transformation. To him, "the life of faith is to be prophetic. And [he] demonstrated that well in his critique of professionalism, his commitment to the poor, his embrace of vocational downward mobility."[39]

It is difficult if not impossible to peg down Henri Nouwen into one exclusive image and role—be it a pastor, a priest, or a prophet—for he assumed a combination of various roles as he ministered to the varying needs of people. Depending on the particular need or situation, Nouwen displayed enormous flexibility in his ministerial style and approach. Nouwen was definitely not one who was chained to any particular role. To insist on rigidly labeling him is nothing but an exercise in futility.

Conversant with a wide variety of soul care and spiritual formation techniques, Nouwen was able to make productive use of their combined elements with creativity and ease. Instinctively, he functioned integratively.

The Wide Spectrum of Soul Nurturance

The contemporary world of Christian soul care and spiritual formation covers an entire gamut of intersecting approaches to spiritual ministry. Soul care by itself alone cuts across the various categories of professional counseling, lay care giving, spiritual guidance and direction, and pastoral care and counseling, to mention some.

In his first comprehensive writing on Christian spirituality, theologian Bruce Demarest does an excellent job addressing the vast array of soul care ministries, including *spiritual friendship, spiritual guidance, spiritual mentoring,* and *spiritual direction.*[40] There is ample evidence, both from his writings and from the accounts of the very people to whom he directly ministered, to suggest that Henri Nouwen utilized all four of these in his own ministry of formation in overlapping ways.

Since Demarest's terms essentially share certain elements and features, it is reasonable to combine them all together under the rubric of "spiritual companioning"—indicative of the sacred accompaniment we cannot do without in our journey. Given that our formative life is irreducibly a communal process, it is quite inconceivable for us to experience soul nurturance apart from this ministry of spiritual companionship.

Soul Companionship

There was never a question at all in Henri Nouwen's mind concerning the benefit of having "a guide, a director, a counselor who helps us to distinguish between the voice of God and all the other voices coming from our own confusion or from dark powers far beyond our control" (RO:137). In his introductory remarks to Kenneth Leech's book *Soul Friend,* Nouwen referred to the danger of traveling without a trusted companion and called attention to the fact that "our way to God is always a human way, and that without a guide our spiritual journey can entangle us in introspective self-preoccupation instead of helping us to become empty for God."[41] All of us can profit from having spiritual companions who can tend to our souls.

In the following two chapters, I will touch on each of the four personalized ministries that Demarest enumerates in his writing. In the process of doing so, I will illustrate, through documented stories of various people, how Henri Nouwen employed these ministries in an integrated way, and for which he is best known.

As a pastoral psychologist and theologian, Nouwen must have certainly engaged in pastoral care and counseling as well. By deliberately narrowing down the concept of soul companioning into four major categories I do not intend to ignore the existence of other equally valid forms of companionship we have available at our disposal today.

For instance, Shalem Institute for Spiritual Formation co-founder Tilden Edwards lists six other types of companionship that are not in and of themselves necessarily mutually exclusive:

Master/Disciple Relationship, Gifted Spiritual Direction, Counseling-Inspired Spiritual Direction, Eldering and Discipling, Informal Relationships, and Mutual Spiritual Direction Relationships.[42] It would not be surprising, therefore, if we discover some of Edwards's classifications intertwining with the four areas I am focusing on. The commonalities somewhat tone down the differences in labeling.

Sticking to Bruce Demarest's categorization, I wish to provide at the outset the most basic definition of each of his four helping ministries. Doing so will enable us to distinguish one from the other without necessarily overlooking their natural interrelationship.

Spiritual friendship, the most informal and reciprocal of all four ministries, involves two or more friends who support, encourage, and pray for one another on their spiritual journeys.

Spiritual guidance refers to general help given individually or in a group—whether in the form of counsel via sermons, letters, or teaching—that seeks to advance the formation of Christlikeness in the other person(s).

Spiritual mentoring is a more formal arrangement in which someone who is more experienced at a given skill teaches, models, and imparts essential knowledge, training, and strategies to someone less experienced.

Spiritual direction refers to the structured ministry of soul care and spiritual formation in which a gifted and experienced Christian helps another person grow in relationship with and obedience to God.

Each of these avenues to *soul companioning* represents a broad spectrum of customized helping ministries aimed toward our spiritual formation in Christ. Without the constraints of a rigid mold, all of them function in elastic and overlapping ways.[43]

CHAPTER TWO

Soul Companion— Friend and Guide

*We need someone who encourages us when we are tempted to
give it all up, to forget it all, to just walk away in despair.
We need someone who discourages us when we move too rashly
in unclear directions or hurry proudly to a nebulous goal.
We need someone who can suggest to us when to read and
when to be silent, which words to reflect upon and what
to do when silence creates much fear and little peace.*
—Henri Nouwen, *Reaching Out*

Not only is it hard but it is also sad to imagine a solitary journey
of the soul. Embarking solo on this journey can also be hazardous
to the health of one's soul. A communal journey is not merely an
option; it is the way it should be. The supportive companionship
of a friend and a guide is never a luxury; it is absolutely essential
for the life of the soul. In Henri Nouwen we have a great example of a friend and a guide combined.

Henri Nouwen as a friend faithfully guided those with whom he connected deeply. As a guide, he reliably directed others along life's journey as only a close friend would, always with the other person's best interest in mind. He was a true friend and has remained a real guide to many through his writings. Henri Nouwen companioned others willingly and eagerly—often as a spiritual friend, at times as a spiritual guide, and on many occasions as both.

Spiritual Friendship

"Friends accompany each other on the journey of life,"[1] says David Benner. Surely, every one of us can use the close companionship of friends on our own journey. Perhaps the real question for us is, "what kind of friends do we really want to have so that we not only survive but flourish in our journey?" We are obviously not talking here of mere "tag along" friends. For the more we embark on our journey, the greater the need for us to have equally deeper friendships to sustain us in the process.

Henri Nouwen knew that somewhat intuitively. He longed and sought for deep, abiding friendships everywhere he went. Nouwen's capacity to connect personally with thousands of friends from various parts of the world is legendary. Of the fifteen hundred people he considered as part of his close circle of friends, he mentioned over six hundred of them by name in the original sabbatical diary he wrote just before he passed away.[2]

For Nouwen, one of the most critical choices we can make in our spiritual life "is the choice of the people with whom we develop close intimate relationships" (*HN*:131). Doubtless, Henri Nouwen placed paramount importance on spiritual friendship. Much of his energy in life was expended making and sustaining friendships with all kinds of people everywhere.

With Aelred of Rievaulx, the gifted Cistercian abbot who penned the classic *Spiritual Friendship,* Nouwen evidently agreed that "friendship from the divine perspective...springs directly from God."[3] As Nouwen himself qualified: "Although we speak of 'making friends,' friends cannot be made. Friends are free gifts from God" (*BJ*: May 1). Both the giver and the receiver mutually share in the gift of spiritual friendship: "It is a gift God gives to us. It is a gift we can give to others."[4]

In evaluating his inner journey, Nouwen recognized very early his own deep need for "regular contact with a friend who keeps [him] close to Jesus and continues to call [him] to faithfulness" (*RD*:208). What Nouwen had in mind is akin to what the Celtic Christians termed *anamchara,* or "soul friend"—"an indispensable companion on the spiritual journey."[5] Celtic believers insisted that a person without a trusted soul friend is like a body without a head. Though by no means the originator of the concept, this ancient group of Christians was responsible for elevating the place of soul friendship to nonnegotiable importance. The experience of having an anamchara was a given for everyone entering the so-called sacred journey.

It is comforting to know that friendships, as Charles Ringma affirms, are there "to help us support one another in common commitments and in the common journey of life."[6] Henri Nouwen took such a commitment to heart. He always was as concerned—if not more concerned—with other people's spiritual journeys as he was with his own. Nouwen's initiatives to move into the lives of others were driven by a genuine desire to be a significant part of their journey with God. As L'Arche founder Jean Vanier has keenly observed, "Henri's cry for friendship and his faithfulness to friendship were particularly evident as he walked with people on their spiritual journeys."[7] So devoted was Nouwen to those whom he considered to be his friends that his very words echo the depth and the breadth of commitment he professed:

> I have lived my whole life with the desire to help others in their journey, but I have always realized that I had little else to offer than my own, the journey I am making myself...I have always wanted to be a good shepherd for others, but I have always known, too, that good shepherds lay down their own lives—their pains and joys, their doubts and hopes, their fears and their love—for their friends. (*GG*:5)

Henri Nouwen was not referring to the act of laying down one's life in a literal fashion. Rather, he meant offering the whole of himself. Nouwen did give of himself to his friends fully without holding anything back.

Henri Nouwen invested much of himself in his co-workers at L'Arche Daybreak, in particular, Sue Mosteller and Nathan Ball. In these friendships we witness how he tried living out—with some success and failure—the core values of friendship he embraced.

MUTUALITY IN FRIENDSHIP

Sue Mosteller and Henri Nouwen first met in 1981, but their formal connection did not begin until five years later when Nouwen accepted the call to be L'Arche community's resident pastor in Toronto, Canada. Out of a shared interest in spirituality, they established a friendship as soon as they began working closely together in the Dayspring House of Prayer.[8]

Sue does not have qualms about painting her friendship with Nouwen as sometimes "complicated." A self-confessed introvert, Sue always had to try to keep pace with Nouwen's extroverted ways. As in any relationship—and partly due to their basic personality differences—Henri and Sue experienced communication gaps. Sometimes they ended up hurting each other in the process, albeit unintentionally. These gaps and the resulting tensions made living in the same community and working together problematic at times.

The tension in their relationship, however, never prevented Sue and Henri from genuinely enjoying a deeper level of friendship characterized by mutual support. They were present to each other at critical junctures in their respective journeying experiences.

Sue recalls a particularly difficult time in her life when she felt burned out and could hardly function normally in her job at L'Arche. Nouwen encouraged her to take some time to get away in order to sort things out. It was also Nouwen who helped her through the feeling of being stuck—when she adamantly refused to go forward with anything. As a friend, Nouwen gently pushed Sue to take risks and go beyond where she wanted to go. Henri and Sue shared many rich moments of vulnerability, thus further strengthening their relationship.

When Nouwen suffered a sudden nervous breakdown fourteen months after coming to L'Arche, it became Sue's turn to offer Nouwen supportive friendship. There was no doubt in both their minds that they could count on each other's support.

All in all, the friendship between Sue and Henri proved to be mutually encouraging for their respective spiritual lives. What they were privileged to engage in was a kind of spiritual friendship that was both purifying and enriching.

Michael O'Laughlin, in his book *Henri Nouwen: His Life and Vision*, describes the enormous role Sue Mosteller played as a true sister in the Lord to Henri Nouwen:

> Henri Nouwen had many close friends, more than anyone has a right to have, but of all these friends it was Sue Mosteller who was entrusted, after his death, with managing his affairs and shaping his legacy. During his last sabbatical, she had taken his place as the community's pastor. Competent and caring, she was a unique person in Henri Nouwen's later years, the one who most challenged and complemented Henri during his life and the one who took up his work when he was gone.[9]

COVENANTAL FRIENDSHIP

Nathan Ball was another very close friend of Henri Nouwen. Nathan and Henri both came to L'Arche Daybreak in 1986. Recalling their many years together, Nathan comments: "Our inner and outer lives would become inexplicably woven as we discovered, individually and together, a call to friendship and a call to become part of the mission of L'Arche that would be lived out in the community of L'Arche Daybreak."[10]

Such recollection is reminiscent of how Aelred of Rievaulx portrays the genuine character of spiritual friendship: one "born of a similarity in life, morals, and pursuits, that is, it is a mutual conformity in matters human and divine united with benevolence and charity."[11] Mutual alignment of lives is the key to true friendship.

From the moment they crossed each other's paths, Henri and Nathan both "experienced an immediate connection of mind and heart." Indeed, a special characteristic of spiritual friends is the depth of mutual sharing at the soul level. Nouwen describes such an experience as "a unity of souls that gives nobility and sincerity to love" (*BJ*:January 7). What drew Nathan and Henri almost instantly together was their "mutual need for friendship that actively supported living a spiritual life." Delightfully they dis-

covered what a true spiritual friend they had in each other—
"someone who so complements [their] spiritual journey that [they find God in a new way through [the other] person."[12]

Of Nouwen's personal impact upon him, Nathan Ball testifies: "[Henri] engaged me in a direct and unabashed manner with the whole of who he was." Moreover, "Henri's insistence that it is not possible to live the spiritual life alone," Nathan admits, "helped call me out from my own place of passivity in relationship to both people and God...We found a bond in this common endeavor of developing a spiritual friendship."

Just like any close relationship absorbed in the challenges of working together, theirs was not exempt from the test of commitment. At one stage, the once well-defined picture of their relationship turned foggy, almost erasing the free nature of what Nathan and Henri both held as a God-given gift.

Slowly, the expectations they had of each other began reaching unrealistic heights. In the process, what started as a mutually empowering relationship ended up to be quite suffocating. This was especially aggravating for Nathan, who always felt at a loss trying to meet Nouwen's unceasing demands for attention and companionship.[13]

Here, Charles Ringma's commentary about the whole realm of expectations as being one of the perennial problems in friendships rings true. He remarks that "while we can expect too little and thus stultify a friendship, we may expect too much and thus put pressure on the relationship that it cannot bear or sustain."[14] Needless to say, this second part of Ringma's comment mirrored exactly what happened to the friendship between Nathan and Henri. Nathan did reach a point where he could no longer give in to Nouwen's dependency and ever-increasing set of expectations. Unfortunately, Nathan's experience was not an isolated one. Jeff Imbach nails it down by commenting that Henri Nouwen's "anguished longing for intimacy and friendship ignited terrible unrest of soul that sometimes played out in needy and manipulative ways."[15]

Nathan Ball's yearning for space led him to distance himself from his relationship with Nouwen. Predictably, Nouwen felt deeply hurt by Nathan's withdrawal and interpreted it as rejection and betrayal. What Nouwen once acknowledged as the "center of

[his] emotional stability" (RD:223) began caving in. The abrupt interruption of their friendship led Nouwen to hit bottom emotionally. A morbid feeling of darkness enveloped his entire being, utterly paralyzing him.[16]

Having reached his threshold of pain, Nouwen became a nervous wreck—a condition that forced him to leave L'Arche and commence serious treatment. He checked into a facility in Winnipeg and remained there for half a year under the spiritual care of a two-person team. This sad episode only dragged into focus what many already knew about Nouwen: his greatest asset also happened to be his greatest liability. Because of his enormous capacity to give to others as well as demand from them attention and affection, friendship for Henri Nouwen was a blessing and a curse.

Almost a decade prior to this unfortunate incident, Nouwen wrote the following thoughts rather prophetically:

No human being can understand us fully, or give us unconditional love, or offer constant affection that enters into the core of our being and heals our deepest brokenness. We know this in our heads but our loneliness pushes us to expect it anyway. When we forget about this profound truth and expect of others more than they can give, we are quickly disillusioned and we easily become resentful, bitter, revengeful, and even violent. (CR:39–40)

Henri Nouwen fell into the very temptation of which he warned others to avoid—entering "an intimacy and closeness that does not leave any open space" since "much suffering results from this suffocating closeness" (CR:40). And Nouwen did suffer much—and so did the precious relationship he had with Nathan Ball. Yet in the grand scheme of things, the suffering itself emerged as a real test.

Fortunately for Henri and Nathan, their friendship stood the test. Following an intense period of spiritual guidance and therapy, Henri Nouwen returned to the community emotionally healed and his relationship with Nathan was eventually restored. Despite the agonizing process involved, the whole episode turned out to be very redemptive for each of them.

Nouwen's experience with Nathan Ball only exposed his own deep wound of loneliness, one that always proved to be rooted in his immense need for love and companionship. Shortly after he wrote his now famous *The Wounded Healer,* Nouwen was quoted in an interview as saying

> I had this idea that loneliness which is pain, when you do not run away from it but feel it through and stand up in it and look it right in the face, that there is something there that can be a source of hope, that in the middle of the pain there is some hidden gift. I, more and more in my life, have discovered that the gifts of life are often hidden in the places that hurt most.[17]

Henri Nouwen openly embraced hope amidst the dark passages he went through in his life. He discovered—and rediscovered—again and again the hidden gifts buried in the most hurtful periods of his existence, including the one he shared with Nathan. His secret journal, which ended up getting published as *The Inner Voice of Love* eight years after the incident with Nathan, chronicled his head-on confrontation with pain and hope wherein "Henri, the wounded healer, speaks to Henri, the wounded person."[18]

Through his most harrowing experience, Nouwen had to learn the hard way what he knew and proclaimed all along: "Friends cannot replace God...But in their limitations they can be signposts on our journey toward the unlimited and unconditional love of God" (*BJ*:May 1). From this divine perspective, spiritual friendship can rightly be viewed as a gift from above. As one writer insightfully points out, friendships "emerge out of the fertile soil of knowing and being known. [They] can help us know ourselves better by mirroring to us the truth of who we are."[19] Such was the stuff of friendship Henri Nouwen indirectly but richly extended to many, including his readers.

Chris Glaser sums up Henri Nouwen's life-shaping experience of the reality of spiritual friendship:

> Henri so desired the "particular friend" discouraged in seminary education and formation and within the priesthood in general!...Jesus became Henri's particular friend. Henri was

yet another "beloved disciple" leaning on Jesus' breast, "listening for the heartbeat of God"...And in turn, Henri became his readers' particular friend.[20]

Spiritual Guidance

Spiritual guidance is another form of spiritual accompaniment, though many regard it as less intimate than spiritual friendship. All the same, it is hard not to correlate it closely with the ministry of friendship. As Henri Nouwen clearly exhibited by example, a true friend is a true guide steering another toward the right path. Conversely, a real guide is just as real as a friend who comes alongside someone in the journeying process.

Spiritual guidance practitioner Carolyn Gratton is correct in emphasizing that the ministry of guidance is itself a work of love, for "to accompany another human person in choosing to follow the invitations of grace is an act of self-giving friendship."[21] On an existential level, therefore, separating friendship from guidance and guidance from friendship can only seem artificial at best.

As a specific type of ministry, spiritual guidance is expressly broad in scope and not as formal and structured as spiritual direction. However, it is not uncommon to see the terms or concepts of *spiritual guidance* and *spiritual direction* used somewhat interchangeably in various literature on soul care and spiritual formation.[22] The way author Howard Rice distinguishes the two is this: spiritual guidance (as a wider category) can employ spiritual direction (as a more exclusive category) with its insights and skills in the same way that pastoral care can draw insights and methods from psychotherapy. Broadly speaking, then, guidance can take place through writing, teaching, or counseling, or even through worship, social change, and management.[23]

In its more qualified sense, spiritual guidance involves "the deliberate attempt to accompany other people on their journeys into God and, in the process, to share what we have learned as we have made our own journeys."[24] The underlying assumption here is that a spiritual guide is a person who possesses a considerable amount of spiritual experience and maturity. Author Marjorie Thompson reinforces this basic assumption by further clarifying that a spiritual guide is one who has traveled some distance along the path of the Christian life. A guide should be knowledgeable about the markers that lead forward on this path, as well as familiar with the pitfalls, detours, trials, and temptations along its course.[25]

In other words, the person must be a veteran traveler, well-acquainted with the terrain of the spiritual journey and all its accompanying realities. Henri Nouwen exemplified perfectly this qualification of a true and effective guide to fellow spiritual travelers.

NOUWEN THE SPIRITUAL GUIDE

Henri Nouwen not only possessed the spiritual ability but also the passionate desire to lead others and show the way. Biblically speaking, that is exactly what a guide does: shows the way (cf. Rom 2:19). Nouwen specifically prayed that his ministry would be "to join people on their journey and to open their eyes to see [the Lord]" (CFM:81). He was convinced that the best thing he could offer others in their journey was the reality of his own journey (GG:4–5). Through the generated wisdom and insights of his writings, Nouwen's personal experiences speak compellingly to his readers. "But as well as writing to guide others, he writes to discover himself," biographer Michael Ford is quick to point out.[26]

Henri Nouwen recognizes spiritual guidance as validating people's essential search for meaning which, to him, inevitably involves our daily experiences in life. Spiritual guidance, he explains, "calls for the creation of space in which the validity of questions does not depend on the availability of answers but on the questions' capacity to open us to new perspectives and horizons." Nouwen further sheds light on the fact that

the quest for meaning can be extremely frustrating and at times even excruciating, precisely because it does not lead to ready answers but to new questions. When we realize that the pain of the human search is a necessary growing pain, we can accept as good the forces of human spiritual development and be grateful for the journey on the long walk of faith.[27]

Well-known author Morton Kelsey situates the ministry of spiritual guidance in a similar context and offers us a good perspective on how to view it more broadly:

> The basic meaning of spiritual guidance is to stand by people in their seeking and searching, in their lostness and despair, in their ugliness and evil (even when they are not aware of their condition). The spiritual guide needs to be open to the darkness, and sometimes to enter it with those whom they guide. And then the guide must produce an environment in which others are open to and transformed by a conquering love greater than most of us have ever imagined.[28]

Interestingly, Kelsey's statements are strikingly similar to Nouwen's abovementioned commentary. Michael Ford concludes: "In a confused and dislocated world, bereft of meaning, Nouwen is a trustworthy companion, even though he admits he does not have all the answers."[29]

Writing about the legacy of Henri Nouwen as a spiritual guide, Deirdre LaNoue notes that "the value of a guide is found in his or her ability to meet you where you are, to understand how you got there, and lead you to where you need to be."[30] In exercising this particular ministry, Henri Nouwen brought the critical elements of spirituality, presence, discernment, creativity, and, most of all, sacred companionship to his role as spiritual guide.

Guidance as a Spiritual Task

Henri Nouwen took the "spiritual" in spiritual guidance seriously. Jean Vanier validates this about Nouwen: "A wise and gentle guide, he led people closer to Jesus, to truth, to a greater acceptance of themselves and of reality" without imposing his faith or his ideas on others.[31] What Nouwen cared most about was to deepen people's spirituality.

Art Laffin could not agree more: "[Henri] was an important spiritual guide, always helping me remember to stay spiritually sustained."[32] Laffin first met Nouwen in 1978 at Yale when he was just starting Covenant Peace Community (CPC), a peace and justice ministry Nouwen heartily endorsed and backed financially. Not only did Nouwen provide spiritual guidance to Laffin but also to the ministry as a whole, urging him and others to keep prayer and community on the forefront of their life of resistance. He often reminded them of the importance of cultivating a vibrant spiritual life amidst their activism.

Henri Nouwen was unwavering in his attention to the spiritual dimension of soul care. He recognized the need "for diagnosticians of the soul who can...guide people to an active and vital transformation of soul and body, and of all their personal relationships"—the ones who promote real change through repentance and faith, confronting and inspiring the people to whom they minister. Nouwen explains the dynamics involved: "Confrontation challenges us to confess and repent; inspiration stirs us to look up again with new courage and confidence" (LR:72, 64). Nouwen exercised both with great care and delicate balance and he guided people always with their spiritual wellbeing as his ultimate concern.

Guidance through Presence

Even beyond his ministerial roles in which speech was so important, Henri Nouwen often evoked a powerful presence to people, whether or not he consciously intended to minister to them. People like Jack Stroh, who personally experienced Nouwen's spiritual guidance, affirms the fact that Nouwen knew exactly how to be present and available to people.[33]

Others, like Joe Vorstermans, interpret Nouwen's often imposing presence in a more intriguing and nuanced way. According to Vorstermans, a longtime member and former lay pastor of L'Arche Daybreak, Nouwen's "complicated presence" can best be understood within the context of what he dubs the "relationship factor." For Nouwen, everything revolved around relationship.

One aspect of Nouwen's eagerness to connect with people—despite his nourishing intent and the quality of vulnerability he offered—stemmed from his own neediness, his insatiable longing for relationship. But the other aspect, which constitutes the best part of him, had to do with his spirit of genuine inclusiveness. Nouwen always wanted to include others, enthusiastically inviting people to enter into a deep, personal relationship with him.[34]

Guidance with Discernment

Far from resorting to a cookie-cutter approach to ministry, Henri Nouwen moved into people's lives with the intent of helping them uncover by themselves their own intimate relationship with God. Since he was so focused on individuals for who they truly were, he was always right on target when it came to the weight of guiding wisdom he dispensed to them.[35]

Alan and Judy Steers, both of whom were affiliated with L'Arche Daybreak over several years in the past, testify that "one of his greatest gifts was the ability to put words to our experience and then show us how God might be seeing that same experience 'from above.'"[36] This observation about Nouwen is similar to Marjorie Thompson's profile of a discerning spiritual guide— "someone who can help us see and name our own experience of God."[37]

Nouwen's capacity to discern wisely was what enabled him to get right to the heart of the matter when confronted with people's issues. A reliable guide, he could point them with certain precision toward the right path because of his own soul's attentiveness to their souls.[38]

Creative Guidance

For Henri Nouwen, guidance is to be looked upon not only as a prophetic form but as a ministerial art as well. A good spiritual guide knows how to creatively guide people by utilizing stories (*LR:65*). As Annice Callahan points out, in guiding people, "[Nouwen] does not preach, but rather he tells...stories."[39] Stories have an inherent healing quality and a transformative effect upon people's lives. Nouwen elaborates on the power of a story as a proven vehicle for offering guidance to people:

> A story that guides is a story that opens a door and offers us space in which to search and boundaries to help us find what we seek, but it does not tell us what to do or how to do it. The story brings us into touch with the vision and so guides us...As long as we have stories to tell to each other there is hope. (*LR:66*)

Through the metaphors and images that constitute stories, we can potentially acquire a newer, fresher way of seeing things—of confronting reality as it is. For it is only when we start seeing with great clarity that life-change even becomes possible. And stories have a way of exposing us to reality and then guiding us in the right direction. In the end, spiritual guidance is mainly about pointing others to the door of hope, which they can choose to open themselves. A companion guide like Nouwen merely paves the way.

Henri Nouwen was a real companion and soul guide. His guidance was inspirational, exemplary, and compelling. As Wendy Greer, past president of the Henri Nouwen Society, articulates:

> [He] has been an inspiring guide for...thousands of people around the world...As a guide he is definitely a companion on the way, gently but persistently urging us to seek an ever closer relationship with God and his son, Jesus Christ.[40]

As a spiritual companion, Nouwen not only assumed the overlapping roles of a soul friend and guide but also took on this approach to spiritual mentoring and direction in his formation ministry.

CHAPTER THREE

Soul Companion— Mentor and Director

Many have quoted the scriptures and many have heard voices and seen visions in silence, but only few have found their way to God...Therefore, we need a guide, a director, a counselor who helps us to distinguish between the voice of God and all the other voices coming from our own confusion or from dark powers far beyond our control.
—Henri Nouwen, *Reaching Out*

Henri Nouwen was a good friend to many people and a close friend to a number of special individuals. As well, he is considered by many as their spiritual guide. To a select few, Nouwen was both a friend to those he guided and a guide to those he befriended. There were also those who looked to Nouwen as their spiritual mentor and/or director, particularly on a one-on-one basis, and he performed these roles with utmost care.

Spiritual Mentoring

Henri Nouwen did not just serve as a friend and guide to many; he mentored specific people in specific ways as well. People were drawn to him for the wealth of wisdom and experience he possessed. For his part, Nouwen was only too willing and eager to share his insights and gifts with those seeking him out for spiritual help. It was in Nouwen's nature to always seek to bring out the best in people. Somehow people picked up that bent of his, and that is why they came to him wanting to learn.

Mentoring can generally be understood as "the process whereby someone who is more experienced at a given skill teaches, models, and imparts essential knowledge, skills, and strategies to someone less experienced."[1] The mentor's standard question to the mentoree is basically, "How can I help you get to where you are going?"[2] This is exactly the kind of question Henri Nouwen would ask the individuals to whom he ministered. His aim was always that people might be freed to be who they were called to be. Herein lies the heart of a real mentor: one of selfless giving for the other's sake.

Authors Keith Anderson and Randy Reese envision the roles of a true spiritual mentor in this light:

> The spiritual mentor is one who comes alongside another for a period of time, brief or extended, in partnership with the Holy Spirit, for the explicit task of nurturing spiritual formation in the life of the mentoree. The one who comes alongside is...capable of *listening, loving, empowering and shining light* on the life of the mentoree (emphasis mine).[3]

The key qualities of a mentor described here by Anderson and Reese mirror the rich and varied ways in which many people perceived Henri Nouwen as a spiritual mentor and experienced him in their lives. In particular, there are three individuals whose stories illustrate different aspects of Nouwen's mentoring style.

A NURTURING RELATIONSHIP

Joe Vorstermans has devoted twenty-eight years of his life to the community of L'Arche Daybreak in Toronto. Ten of these he spent working closely with Henri Nouwen as his mentor. Joe, who assumed the role of lay pastor at L'Arche community after Nouwen's untimely death, points to his friendship with Nouwen as foundational in developing their mentoring relationship. In affirmation of this vital foundation, spiritual theologian James Houston remarks that "spiritual mentors matter most when the spiritual life is centered upon spiritual friendships."[4]

A Mentor-Friend

Joe remembers how Nouwen became a mentor-friend, counseling him during the different stages of his married life.[5] When his relationship with his wife at some point became shaky and he felt as if he were losing hope, Nouwen provided much-needed hope. Joe was especially impressed by Nouwen's incredible "capacity to trust that pain would be redeemed by new life." Not only did Nouwen support but he also empowered Joe in his role as a pastor-in-training. As Joe gratefully recalls, "[Henri] also saw gifts in me that I could not recognize and invited me to work with him in pastoral situations."[6]

Nouwen was likewise generous in providing all the necessary resources for Joe to succeed in his job and was very accepting of Joe's limitations. Even when Nouwen felt disappointed at times with how some events turned out that were not consistent with his expectations, he never got stuck and held anything against Joe—something that Joe considers as an antithesis of his experience with his father, who placed high and oftentimes impossible expectations on him. Not that Nouwen was any less demanding, but in their working relationship together, Nouwen was careful not to let any potentially crippling job-related issues get in the way and slow down their normal functioning. He made sure that both he and Joe were always quick to pick up and move forward.[7]

In many ways, Joe Vorstermans looked up to Nouwen as a father figure, admiring in particular his pastoral and informal demeanor. Most specially, he appreciated Nouwen's genuine interest in and attentiveness to him as an individual. With Nouwen, Joe experienced a genuinely nurturing relationship that he never felt toward his earthly father.[8]

A Fearless and Faithful Mentor

As a mentor, Joe found in Nouwen an amazing ability to meet people in their own place. He was able to focus on their specific issues while at the same time situate everything in a much broader spiritual context. This larger perspective employed by Nouwen so influenced Joe that it radically changed even the way he viewed the person of Nouwen along with his idiosyncratic "issues."

For example, Joe, like many others, sometimes felt that Nouwen's relational initiatives could be a bit intrusive. Initially, Joe interpreted Nouwen's moves toward him as an outright invasion of space. In retrospect, Joe now sees beyond all that. When asked to identify Nouwen's lingering impact upon him as a mentor, it is Nouwen's fearlessness that first comes to mind. "Henri unhesitatingly moved into my life," Joe recounts, "and the risks he made only resulted in my own growth and development as a person."

Another quality of Henri Nouwen that made a deep impression on Joe was his lived-out faithfulness to God and to others. These two spiritual values that Nouwen modeled before Joe—fearlessness and faithfulness—have become so ingrained in his consciousness that he feels as though Nouwen's spirit truly lives on.

Nouwen's spirit has so overwhelmingly captured Joe that even now he finds himself living by the same conviction of fearlessness and faithfulness—though not so much in the identical "form" by which Nouwen displayed it, but more in the "spirit" behind the form. In this manner, Joe feels freer to be himself as opposed to being a mere carbon copy of his esteemed mentor.[9]

A LOVING PRESENCE AND ATTENTIVENESS

The one thing that stands out for Andrew Kennedy in his recollection of Henri Nouwen is his unpretentiousness when it came to his concern for people. He himself was overwhelmed by Nouwen's loving concern. Nouwen entered Kennedy's world and acted as his spiritual mentor during a miserably low period in his life, triggered by the suicide of his brother Michael.

Andrew vividly recalls his first encounter with Nouwen: "He consumed me when I spoke. The intensity of his focus was so strong, it was though nothing else in the world existed for him during a conversation."[10] This documented episode is but one of the many tributes to Nouwen's immense capacity not just for attentive but also compassionate listening. Kathy Christie, Nouwen's personal secretary during the last four years of his life, confirms that Nouwen's "ability to really listen" was one of Nouwen's outstanding gifts to people.[11]

Siobhan Keogh also singles out Henri Nouwen's overpowering intensity as one of his most outstanding qualities. As she expounds on it in her own words, "Henri's intensity has much to do with his relentless interest in the truth. You can watch his eyes peer into you, wanting to get you into the truth of who you are. Then he challenges you to move into those inner places where you don't want to go yourself."[12]

Henri Nouwen's listening capacity was nothing short of phenomenal. He not only knew how to listen attentively; he listened lovingly and compassionately as well. In Beth Porter's words, "Always he modeled a compassionate attentiveness."[13] This was how he managed to establish such a powerful connection with so many people. To Nouwen, listening as "a form of spiritual hospitality" meant "paying full attention to others and welcoming them into our very beings" (*BJ*:March 11).

Andrew Kennedy must have felt this type of hospitality from Nouwen and felt it deeply enough to set him on the path of his own transformation. Andrew Kennedy's story remains one of the most moving accounts of how one life can be so transformed by God through the avenue of an attentive mentoring relationship.

A MENTOR'S EMPOWERMENT

Among the many grateful beneficiaries of Henri Nouwen's mentoring ministry is Wendy Lywood, an Anglican (Episcopal) priest serving as the sacramental minister at L'Arche Daybreak. Brimming with thankfulness, Wendy shares how "Henri gave [her] an incredible gift, one that many people long to receive..., the gift of having a mentor." For her, "Henri was...a role model, a teacher, a pastor, a priest, and a companion on the human journey."[14]

At a critical point in Wendy's journey, when she wallowed in self-doubt about her vocational identity and was on the brink of losing hope, Nouwen enabled her to make sense of her experience by opening up the word to her. Nouwen urged Wendy to go forward with her life by calling her back into her priesthood.[15] In retrospect, Wendy attests: "Henri's mentoring helped me to open up my life to receive the gifts of peace, joy, hope, courage, confidence, and lots of trust."[16] At the heart of Wendy Lywood's experience with Henri Nouwen lay the relational dynamic that is central to the mentoring enterprise.

Dynamics of Spiritual Mentoring

Wendy Lywood's testimony of her experience with Nouwen's mentorship is very much in accord with the five dynamics involved in spiritual mentoring—first identified by J. Robert Clinton and that Anderson and Reese adapted as the framework of discussion in their book *Spiritual Mentoring*. In brief, the five interactive movements in the spiritual mentoring process are: *attraction* (establishing a mentoring relationship), *relationship* (nurturing trust and intimacy), *responsiveness* (sustaining a responsive spirit), *accountability* (refining growth through accountable disciplines), and *empowerment* (facilitating the discovery of one's unique voice for kingdom service).[17]

In tangible and concrete ways, these movements resemble closely the journey Wendy went through with Henri Nouwen. Let us examine briefly how each stage correlates with Wendy's specific context and situation.[18]

Attraction. Having read and familiarized herself with many of Nouwen's writings and watched his way of life closely in their shared community, Wendy was automatically drawn to seek out Nouwen as a mentor.

Relationship. With the opportunity of not only working together but also praying regularly with Nouwen as well as witnessing him live out his full humanness before the entire community, Wendy found it easy to connect with Nouwen and develop a growing relationship of trust in him.

Responsiveness. Through Nouwen's persistent encouragement side by side with his commitment to seize every teaching moment for Wendy's sake, Wendy was afforded lots of opportunities to rise to the occasion and learn to more boldly speak from her own relationship with God.

Accountability. In very specific instances, Nouwen made sure that Wendy was thrust into more visible pastoral roles and situations by giving her regular responsibilities that fostered a sense of accountability such as doing the Eucharist reflections, joining the pastoral team for hospital visitations, and the like.

Empowerment. Nouwen wisely facilitated Wendy's continued personal and professional growth by allowing her to find her own voice, culminating with the rediscovery of her own calling into the priesthood.

Wendy Lywood's story wonderfully illustrates what authentic spiritual mentoring looks like. Contrary to the ill-conceived notion of a rigidly tight and highly controlled mentoring relationship—the kind guaranteed to produce clones out of mentorees—real mentoring is liberating. Good mentors release mentorees to be their own person, empowering them to live out their true identity.

The Goal of Spiritual Mentoring

Empowerment is the ultimate goal of true spiritual mentoring. "The spirit of the mentoring relationship," according to Bruce Demarest, "is that the mentor imparts...things freely, in order to help the protégés attain goals that are their own." Demarest hastens to add that "it is not mentoring, but something else, if we try to recreate people in our own image, or to accomplish goals that are ours, not theirs."[19] Drawing from the well-crafted words of Anderson and Reese,

> a healthy mentoring relationship should help you to give voice to the song God has sung into your life, to liberate the song that has lain dormant or imprisoned in your history. You should be able to sing the song with your own voice, in your own way, as a response of joy to the amazement of hearing God sing to you. Through spiritual mentoring you will freely and vigorously exercise your God-given gifts in a ministry that is equally God-given. You will discover the voice within and let ring out![20]

Henri Nouwen paved the way for this reality to take place in Wendy Lywood's experience. Likewise Nouwen fulfilled this same goal for Joe Vorstermans even as Joe learned to reclaim his uniqueness and continue to stand on his own especially after Nouwen's permanent absence from his familiar world.

This only shows the kind of selfless commitment Henri Nouwen extended to those unto whom he ministered. Along the same vein, Siobhan Keogh articulates Nouwen's greatest impact upon her personally: "Henri has always insisted on me recognizing my own path. Even more so, he has urged me continually to keep following my unique path."[21] Nouwen was really not after advancing his agenda; he was devoted instead to empowering others.

Parker Palmer, the famed educator, wrote this short piece in his journal in loving memory of Henri Nouwen, his mentor and friend:

> Henri's spirit continues to call me...to more openness and vulnerability, more shared humanity and mutual healing, even—and perhaps especially—when the subject is so difficult that words seem to fail.[22]

This is but a sample of Nouwen's lingering relational influence via his ministry of mentoring. In depicting Nouwen's overall mentoring impact, Ronald Rolheiser could not have phrased it better:

> By sharing his own struggles, he mentored us all, helping us to pray while not knowing how to pray, to rest while feeling restless, to be at peace while tempted, to feel safe while still anxious, to be surrounded by a cloud of light while still in darkness, and to love while still in doubt.[23]

Henri Nouwen was not just a mentor; he was a mentor-friend. As a mentor-friend, he offered wise guidance necessary to direct others to their own chosen path. On many occasions, Nouwen likewise functioned as a sensitive, discerning spiritual director.

Spiritual Direction

Of the four dimensions of soul care and spiritual formation mentioned, *spiritual direction* is the most favored term that enjoys good press in contemporary spirituality circles. A renaissance is in fact taking place at the start of the twenty-first century regarding the ministry of spiritual direction, giving way to various intriguing trends.[24] However, along with the more popularized designation of spiritual direction comes some rhetoric—at times obscuring instead of clarifying its basic concept for the layperson.

Our chief concern is not to peg down our terms with exactness. Whatever term of preference is employed—*spiritual counsel, spiritual guidance, soul friendship,* or *spiritual direction*—we do not want to miss the point: they are all intended means and processes of soul care and spiritual formation. They are all designed for "companionship" which, as Alan Jones metaphorically describes, is "for the hatching of our hearts," that is, "for the bringing home of our scattered and fragmented selves, for the making of a heart at home with itself."[25]

Nevertheless, *spiritual direction* still holds the time-honored distinction of being the most ancient term directly identified with the long established history of the cure of souls. Its modern-day rediscovery represents for many "the recovery of the lost jewel in the crown of Christian soul care."[26]

SPIRITUAL DIRECTION ACCORDING TO NOUWEN

Henri Nouwen seized the practice of spiritual direction for his own sake and for the sake of others. He sought direction for himself when he needed it and gave direction to others who asked for it. Creatively, he was able to draw from its rich diversity of expressions while at the same time wisely focusing on its most fundamental thrust: listening to God.

As if to wipe out its rhetorical mist and in the process demystifying it, Henri Nouwen—in his characteristic simplicity—boiled down his definition of spiritual direction to that of "direction given to people in their relationship with God."[27] God is the ultimate focus of spiritual direction. It is not just a one-on-one but a one-with-one encounter. For Nouwen, "a spiritual director simply was someone who talks to you and prays with you about your life."[28] Nouwen focused on this critical component of prayer, which is the lifeblood of any true spiritual direction relationship.

The Dynamic of Prayer

At the heart of the spiritual direction experience is the dynamic of prayer. Henri Nouwen paints the profile of a spiritual director as a mature person "from whom we can expect prayerful guidance in our constant struggle to discern God's active presence in our lives."[29] As he explains further, "the prayer life of the spiritual director is the source of his or her own directing ministry. To be a spiritual director means to share one's prayer with the searching other."[30]

Lorenzo Sforza-Cesarini, who is a member of L'Arche Daybreak's pastoral team, confirms this focus through his own experience of spiritual direction with Nouwen. "The process Henri guided me through had prayer as its center," he points out.[31] Indeed, prayer is "the beginning and end of all spiritual assistance," Nouwen stresses. The concentration of the director's ministry itself rests on the prayer life of the directee.[32]

Conversational Prayer

Henri Nouwen regards prayer as "an outward, careful attentiveness to the One who invites us to an unceasing conversation."[33] It involves not only the presentation but more so the conversion of our thoughts into conversational prayer, thus moving us "from a self-centered monologue to a God-centered dialogue."[34]

Prayer is our response to God's overtures of love, his initiatives and inner promptings. It becomes an avenue by which we connect with God and seek to cooperate with his already active work in our lives. In a specific way this is given solid expression during a spiritual direction session when the director engages in praying to God for and with the directee conversationally.

Contemplative Prayer

Prayer is not only conversation but contemplation as well. Fundamentally, Henri Nouwen believes "prayer is an attitude of open heart, silently in tune with the Spirit of God, revealing itself in gratitude and contemplation."[35] In saying this he notes the primary thrust of prayer is that of listening and waiting. He elaborates:

> We listen for God in an attitude of openness of heart, humility of spirit, and quietness of soul. We let our mind descend into our heart and there stand in the presence of God.[36]

Contemplation engages our inner capacity to peer into and through the center of reality (*GD*:36–37). Through contemplative prayer we are enabled to see people and things more transparently in our direction experience.

The Role of Discernment

Directly related to the centrality of prayer—conversational as well as contemplative—is the crucial aspect of discernment. As we learn to dialogue more openly with God and contemplate his presence, we start to see more clearly the process of discernment—being attuned to God's movements.

Cultivating a discerning heart has much to do with the development of that all-important trait all spiritual directors must possess—being a sensitive listener. Henri Nouwen brings to our attention the reality that true spiritual direction "means that...people come together to listen to the direction of the Spirit."[37] The Holy Spirit must be acknowledged ultimately to be the real director.

Father Damien Isabell, editor of the *Journal of the Midwest Association of Spiritual Directors*, remarks:

> A spiritual director is one who helps a fellow Christian to search his heart for the Holy Spirit who is leading him towards fullness of life. Part of the challenge of direction is the discernment of this elusive Spirit through the human prism of emotion, passion, history and desire. *Henri Nouwen has the unique gift of being able to peer through that prism to the very source of light and darkness* (emphasis mine).[38]

Susan Zimmerman confirms this about her experience as a directee of Nouwen: "Henri's genius lay in his capacity to confront the unexamined material of everyday life, the material...[lying] unconsciously just below the surface of our daily relationships." Impressed by Nouwen's focusing skills, Susan concludes: "[Nouwen's] insight could cut incisively through layers of confusion."[39]

Lisa Cataldo also connects with a similar experience with Henri Nouwen. During spiritual direction with him, Lisa repeatedly voiced her feeling of being torn between what she felt as her strong calling to the Episcopal priesthood and her deep attachment to her Roman Catholic roots. As one whose fierce commitment in life was to be able to view every situation she faced in black or white and interpret it in an either-or fashion, Lisa struggled to live with tension—a tendency Nouwen was only too quick to catch. "Henri saw straight to the heart of the matter. He saw all my experiences as 'stones in the road' of my spiritual journey," she reports. Nouwen helped Lisa get beyond her issue by pointing her to the *real* issue: pursuing the "known" and leaving to God the "unknown."[40]

In reminiscing about her brief but eye-opening episodes with Nouwen, Lisa Cataldo still admires Nouwen's intuitive mode of listening and discerning. "Henri listened in a spiritual way. He didn't just listen to my words; he was able to see underneath and beyond those words. He heard at a level much deeper than words. Nouwen instinctively heard even what was not said." Lisa remains convinced that Nouwen truly possessed a rare gift of discernment.[41]

Prayer and Discernment

Prayer and discernment are the twin dynamics that elevate spiritual direction to its unique status as a highly personalized ministry of soul care and spiritual formation. No exercise of spiritual direction can ever be fruitful without these two nonnegotiable elements at work. As Henri Nouwen emphasizes, spiritual direction "offers prayerful presence, wise counsel, and careful guidance by a spiritual friend who is sensitive to the movements of the Spirit."[42] In short, everything about spiritual direction revolves around prayer and discernment. In it, we pray as we discern and discern as we pray.

What made Henri Nouwen the effective spiritual director that he was can largely be attributed to the fact that he refused to stray from these two focal points; instead, he relied heavily on the Spirit's work to use the crucial avenues of prayer and discernment to effect inner change in people's lives.[43] He prayed and discerned out of a deep motivation in his heart to see this change take place.

NOUWEN THE SPIRITUAL DIRECTOR

The prospect of inner transformation in people was for the most part what energized Henri Nouwen's work of spiritual direction. His efforts did not prove to be in vain. "The greatest gift...that Henri left me was a profound renewal of my spiritual life," Siobhan Keogh says soberly.[44] Now without Nouwen, she is left to rely on her own determination to follow the path of spirituality Nouwen forged for her. Siobhan, who sought Nouwen as spiritual director in 1987, testifies about her revitalized life—"a life where I became in touch with my spirit...to claim my unique identity and my unique journey."[45]

For Lisa Cataldo, it was all about trusting God—that he has something for her to do. The basic question of what to do next is no longer a huge matter of concern but of trust. When it comes to the issue of vocation, Lisa has learned to not try and figure things out on her own but instead to trust her own sense of call, to trust herself and her unique experience of God. This fundamental lesson of trust has changed Lisa's entire perspective on her vocation and has given her much peace of mind amidst the perennial uncertainties of life. Lisa now feels more secure and at rest knowing God is in control and she is not.[46]

Henri Nouwen's authentic love for people was extraordinary. As a spiritual director, he lived out the truth of what it means to be a true companion along another's journey. One of his longtime co-workers at L'Arche personally certifies: "Henri really wanted to know what my spiritual journey was about, what my turning points were, what was going on inside me."[47] Nouwen's interest in others was refreshingly genuine.

For Andrew Dreitcer, it was Henri Nouwen's "way of being" that has profoundly influenced how he has come to conceive the reality of the spiritual life. Insofar as he was concerned, Nouwen never came across as being dogmatic. His approach was consistently more of a probing, curious, and open-ended posture. Nouwen formed and informed Dreitcer's own ministry approach—which is one of utmost respect for other people's unique journeying reality.[48]

Finally, Andrew Dreitcer rounds off Nouwen's enduring impact as a spiritual minister based upon his experience with him at Yale when he, together with eleven other students, took a class on group spiritual direction during the fall of 1980: "We learned about spiritual direction primarily because Henri modeled it for us. He showed us how to be the spiritual friend, the sacred companion. He offered us the space and time to be companions to one another."[49]

Andrew Dreitcer's words simply but compellingly sum up the kind of versatile journey companion Henri Nouwen was to many people. He filled the oftentimes indistinguishable roles of a spiritual friend, a spiritual guide, a spiritual mentor, and a spiritual director effortlessly. He was able to do so because this was precisely who he was—a well-integrated soul companion on life's sacred journey.

CHAPTER FOUR

A Ministry of Integration

*Real ministry starts taking place when we bring others
in touch with more than we ourselves are—the center of
being, the reality of the unseen—the Father who is
the source of life and healing.*
—Henri Nouwen, *Turn My Mourning into Dancing*

Henri Nouwen employed the broad spectrum of soul care and
spiritual formation ministries in both situated as well as integrated modes. Still, one wonders whether Nouwen was consciously aware of—or if he even cared to define—what ministry
role he assumed at different times and in different contexts with
different people. It is probably not far-fetched to assume that
Nouwen must have combined various roles instinctively.

More than likely, the people themselves who received
Nouwen's ministry defined his role according to whether they felt
ministered to as a friend, counselee, mentee, or directee. It may
even be true that some people experienced Nouwen in his multiple, overlapping roles. For instance, Michael Christensen claimed

Nouwen primarily as his mentor and guide while at the same time experiencing him at various junctures in his journey as a teacher, a priest, a spiritual director, and a close spiritual friend.[1] In any case, there is no doubt that Henri Nouwen ministered integratively. The question is, what are the key dynamics involved?

Integrated Dynamics of Spiritual Formation

Henri Nouwen's spiritual ministry of formation, although multifaceted, was highly unified and dynamically integrated. His locus of integration hinged on his comprehensive and nuanced understanding of the intricate but nonetheless seamless interrelationship of spirituality with psychology, ministry, and theology.

Whether operating in his capacity as a pastor, priest, or prophet, or functioning as a spiritual friend, guide, mentor, or director, or any other ministry role for that matter, Henri Nouwen ministered integratively. Nouwen's concept of the spiritual life and its formation is itself wholly integrated.

What fundamentally informed and formed Henri Nouwen's own journey of integration as an individual was the coinherent view of spirituality to which he subscribed. The philosophical framework he embraced gave way to the kind of methodological approach to ministry that he consequently practiced. Thus, it could be said that Henri Nouwen's spirituality of integration very much dictated the shape of his ministry of spiritual formation, which is essentially about a ministry of integration.

The key dynamics involved in Henri Nouwen's integrated work fall under the three major areas that coincide with spirituality's coinherence with psychology, ministry, and theology. Furthermore, patterned after Nouwen's ministry that is simultaneously integrative, counterintuitive, and countercultural in nature, we hope to glean vital implications and practical applications related to how we ourselves can do ministry.

PSYCHOLOGICAL AND SPIRITUAL DYNAMICS

As noted earlier, when referring to the reality of the soul we are in essence also representing the self since both are ontologically substantive in their formation and development. Thus, we identify the soul and/or self interchangeably to mean the totality of the person created in the image of God. In conjunction with this under-standing, we can speak of soul care as self-care and equate both with the notion of spiritual care. The reason for this lies in the fact that the self is inherently spiritual in its core identity.

The Self's Spiritual Identity

Henri Nouwen emphasizes the reality that "we are not who we know ourselves to be, but who we are known to be by God."[2] Our real identity is the one that is defined by God—a creation made in God's own image. When therefore we speak of our spir-itual identity, we are really referring to our true self—"the self that [we are] called to be from the dawn of eternity."[3]

Our spiritual constitution of our identity is underscored by the manner in which we connect with our true self. In C. S. Lewis's instructive words, "Your real...self...will not come as long as you are looking for it. It will come when you are looking for him."[4] Phrased differently, David Benner reiterates, "We do not find our true self by seeking it. Rather, we find it by seeking God. For...in finding God we find our truest and deepest self."[5]

The fact that there is such a thing as the true self implies that there is likewise the potent existence of the false self—something already alluded to in chapter 1. Psychologist R. D. Laing referred to it as "one way of not being oneself" or a way of living inauthenti-cally.[6] The way Basil Pennington explains its outworking, the false self attaches itself to things while remaining detached from God.[7]

Biblically speaking, Kenneth Boa identifies the false or old self with Paul's use of *sarx* (the flesh), which always struggles for autonomy from God.[8] What Paul describes as "life according to the flesh," or "flesh life," is actually "the pervasively self-referenced life of the false self."[9] Robert Mulholland explicitly labels it as a fearful, protective, possessive, manipulative, destructive, self-promoting, indulgent, distinction-making self.[10] Part of the spiri-tual journey of the self involves the soul work of confronting and arresting the maneuverings of the false self.

Spiritual Journey of the Self

Scripture makes clear that the end goal of our journey has to do with our conformity with Christ (Rom 8:29). The journey of the self therefore points to the lifelong process of us becoming our true self in Christ. Theologian Ellen Charry puts it this way: "Our true identity is reclaimed for us by God in Christ so that we may return to our proper self"[11]—which is to say, our true, original self. This is why the self that starts on the journey is never the same self that finally arrives.[12]

One way of conceiving this journey of the self is to set it against the backdrop of the familiar biblical drama involving *creation, fall, redemption,* and the *eschaton* (the future consummation of things). In creation, we all started with our true self, bearing the image and likeness of God (Gen 1:26). In the fall, because of sin, humans ended up becoming fallen image bearers, turning their true self into a false self (Rom 3:23). Fortunately, there is the stage of redemption, where in Christ we receive a new self that enables us to return to our real self at the eschaton (2 Cor 3:18; 1 John 3:2).[13]

Our ability or inability to grasp our true spiritual identity is bound to affect our self-identity and consequently our ministry—positively or negatively.

The Minister's Self-Identity

The self-identity of the minister is a central issue in Christian ministry and is of particular concern in the field of pastoral care and counseling.[14] Henri Nouwen understood well its vital importance. Whether as a pastor, counselor, spiritual director, or any kind of soul care provider, the minister discovers that his or her identity is a crucial factor in being effective.

Living "from the center of our being, where our identity is defined by God, not others," Nouwen points out, is what enables us to care and thus minister with real depth and effectiveness.[15] Therefore, we can only minister out of who we are. If we are not secure in our own identity, our inner instability is bound to exude a negative impact in the way we minister to people. For us to be able to affect others in a deeply positive way, we need constantly to claim our true self in Christ.

Reclaiming One's Identity

It took a transcendent encounter with the mystical for Henri Nouwen to be forced to confront and reestablish his own identity as a person of faith. The unusual experience transpired while he was about to undergo surgery in 1989 as a result of his near brush with death. Reminiscing in detail the eye-opening experience in which he found himself immersed prior to his surgery, Nouwen shared the following revelation:

> What I experienced then was something I had never experienced before: pure and unconditional love. Better still, what I experienced was an intensely personal presence, a presence that pushed all my fears aside and said, "Come, don't be afraid. I love you." (*BM*:33)

Henri Nouwen's profound experience of the reality of God's love was what empowered him to proclaim his identity with such renewed conviction: "I am a child of God, a brother of Jesus. I am held safe in the intimacy of the divine love." Nouwen applied to himself the very words spoken by God to Jesus: "This is my beloved Son, with whom I am well pleased" (Matt 3:17). The true identity of Jesus as God's beloved, Nouwen realized, was also his to rightfully claim (*BM*:68).

As one constantly plagued by bouts of self-rejection and self-depreciation, Nouwen confessed to struggling with the truth of his identity. Once he grasped more deeply the essence of his belovedness, he then felt freer to give of himself in love to others. Propelled by such a life-transforming perspective, Nouwen confessed:

> The great spiritual task facing me is to so fully trust that I belong to God that I can be free in the world—free to speak even when my words are not received; free to act even when my actions are criticized, ridiculed, or considered useless; free also to receive love from people and to be grateful for all the signs of God's presence in the world. I am convinced that I will truly be able to love the world when I fully believe that I am loved far beyond its boundaries. (*BM*:69–70)

Henri Nouwen's effectiveness to reach out in love to the world was directly contingent upon the extent to which he allowed God's love to reach in to the very depths of his experience. Michael O'Laughlin commented: "Henri's personal spirituality"—as well as his effective, well-integrated ministry—"revolved around his realizing and embracing his own identity."[16]

The Art of Self-Utilization

For Henri Nouwen, then, "self affirmation and self-emptying are not opposites because no man can give away what he does not have" (*CM*:51, 52). You cannot empty something you do not even recognize as ontologically existing—such as your *self*. You can use your self to bless other people only after you have identified and recognized the blessing that is truly your self. Self-identification is a precondition to self-utilization.

Deeply rooted in the Clinical Pastoral Education (CPE) movement, "the concept of the utilization of the self in ministry has become fully ensconced in the field of pastoral care."[17] Henri Nouwen skillfully modeled this concept by capitalizing on the image of the "wounded healer" as his guiding image.

Self-Knowledge and Self-Awareness

Pastoral care theorist Alastair Campbell builds upon this same image popularized by Nouwen and elevates the absolute necessity of self-knowledge in order to utilize the self effectively. Campbell insists, "We must learn to know our fears, our wounds and our foolishness, and to know them in quite specific ways."[18] It is true that only through honest self-exploration that leads to greater self-awareness—which consequently breeds self-respect— can a minister be empowered to minister to others more productively.[19] According to Henri Nouwen, there has to be a serious reaching in to one's innermost being prior to reaching out to others.

Self-knowledge and self-awareness in relation to God are indispensable media through which we can reach out more sensitively to others. Nouwen reminds us that

> we will never be able to really care if we are not willing to paint and repaint constantly our self-portrait, not as a morbid self-preoccupation, but as a service to those who are searching for some light in the midst of the darkness.[20]

Not too many ministers possess a good portrait, let alone an accurate and realistic one, of themselves. Part of truly caring for and serving others is by being true to one's self.

Sadly, for many of us, our true self is often masked heavily by the endless trappings of our many false selves. We must keep discarding our false self so that the real one can come out unhindered. The real one is the only one worth giving away.

One sure way that we can paint and repaint our self-portrait is to utilize the search light of the Spirit and in solitude and silence continually beseech God in prayer the way the psalmist David did: "Search me, O God, and know my heart; test me and know my thoughts. See if there is any wicked way in me" (Ps 139:23–24a).

Self-Disclosure and Self-Portrayal

Self-disclosure and self-portrayal represent two fruitful means of utilizing the self.[21] We know from Henri Nouwen's revealing journals and diaries how he maximized these particular means in ways that benefited his readers greatly. His books have served as effective vehicles by which people have gained free access to his inner person: "My books…are from someone always searching, wondering. I trust my struggle is not just for me. It is given to me for others too."[22]

This type of access to Nouwen via his written works has proven again and again to be freeing for many because of the instant connection people find in Nouwen's transparent portrayal of himself. For in his portrayal of himself, they always end up seeing clearly their own version of themselves so glaringly mirrored before them. Henri Nouwen is one of the few who could powerfully "articulate a vulnerability that people embraced."[23]

The Power of Storytelling

One other proven vehicle in connection with self-utilization is the creative art of storytelling, which Henri Nouwen took full advantage of in his ministry. Nouwen opened himself up to others as a way of ministering through the subtle but compelling medium of stories. He enumerates the outstanding qualities inherent in the telling of a story:

It creates space. We can dwell in a story, walk around, find our own place. The story confronts but does not oppress; the story inspires but does not manipulate. The story invites us to an encounter, a dialog, a mutual sharing. (*LR*:65–66)

More important, stories possess healing power. It is through "the receiving and full understanding of the story" that healing occurs. Thus, Nouwen advises us, "we have to receive the story of our fellow human beings with a compassionate heart, a heart that does not judge or condemn but recognizes how the [other's] story connects with our own" (*RO*:96). Through the transparent sharing of our stories, we are able to express our care more tangibly even as we willingly offer our "own vulnerable self to others as a source of healing."[24] Doing so also "can lead to a new self-understanding, but this...can never be its own goal. We are for others."[25]

Henri Nouwen was a man for others. He gave unreservedly of himself because he had a full self to give, a self anchored upon his true, spiritual identity before God as God's beloved (*BJ*:June 3). Therefore, Nouwen could minister as one who "had the authority of clarity, vulnerability, and truth...[and] was able to do what Jesus did—to take the smallest encounters, the simplest experiences, and the most common human flaws, and cast them in a light which revealed them as vehicles for the grace of God."[26] In ministry, you can only give what you have—and who you are.

Henri Nouwen was effective in his ministry of spiritual care giving because he knew who he was as a minister. Clearly, he comprehended that one's self-identity is ultimately based upon one's true spiritual identity. Thus, the more he embraced that truth and claimed it for himself, the more empowered he felt to extend himself to others in ministry. Ministry is precisely that—"the giving of self" (*GI*:85).

Henri Nouwen administered the care of the soul as the care of the spirit to the people he understood to be integrated psychospiritual beings. The natural blending of the psychological with the spiritual in Henri Nouwen's ministry dynamics no doubt enhanced his effectiveness as a minister.

In the same way, Nouwen also did not separate the dynamics between spirituality and ministry. He engaged them both as an integrated piece and uncovered its reciprocal and cyclical dynamics.

SPIRITUAL AND MINISTERIAL DYNAMICS

Henri Nouwen's ministry of spirituality was manifestly inseparable from his spirituality of ministry. His familiar themes of
solitude, community, and ministry can be recast in a more expan-
sive way as *communion, community,* and *commission,* for easy
recall, and then analyzed for their dynamic interrelationships.

In the familiar New Testament account found in Luke 6:12–19,
we observe Jesus establishing the true and proper sequence for spiritual ministry—a clear movement from solitude to community
and to ministry.[27]

> Now during those days he went out to the mountain to
> pray; and he spent the night in prayer to God. And when
> day came, he called his disciples and chose twelve of them,
> whom he also named apostles: Simon, whom he named
> Peter, and his brother Andrew, and James, and John, and
> Philip, and Bartholomew, and Matthew, and Thomas, and
> James son of Alphaeus, and Simon, who was called the
> Zealot, and Judas son of James, and Judas Iscariot, who
> became a traitor. He came down with them and stood on a
> level place, with a great crowd of his disciples and a great
> multitude of people from all Judea, Jerusalem, and the coast
> of Tyre and Sidon. They had come to hear him and to be
> healed of their diseases; and those who were troubled with
> unclean spirits were cured. And all the crowd were trying to
> touch him, for power came out from him and healed all of
> them.

We are informed, first of all, that Jesus spent the entire night
communing with God in prayer. When morning came, he sum-
moned his disciples together and designated twelve of them to be
his apostles. Afterward during that same day, Jesus, with his chosen apostles, went out to the multitudes and preached the gospel
and healed the sick.

Henri Nouwen freely applied the symbolism of *night, morning,* and *afternoon* to this passage to dramatize the sequential pattern of the spiritual life, which "begins in solitude at night, moves
to community building in the morning, and ends in active ministry in the afternoon."[28]

The same pattern unfolds in the Gospel of Mark, where we are told that Jesus "appointed the twelve...that they might be *with* him and that he might send them out to preach" (3:14 NIV, emphasis mine). The call to be with Christ is an invitation to *communion*. That it is not merely an individual but a corporate call speaks loudly of the vital role of *community*. Out of this process of being in communion with Jesus and experiencing community with each other comes the Lord's *commission* to go out to all the world and preach the good news, thus perpetuating the same cycle of communion, community, and commission with and through others. Let us now look closely at each process and then pinpoint the cyclical dynamics in each of them.

Communion

Communion means to be in abiding union with God, who designed each of us for that exact purpose (*HN*:43). In simplest terms, it is to be with and to stay in God's divine presence. In the metaphorical language of John the apostle, it means being attached to the Vine, without which we can do nothing (John 15:5). For Henri Nouwen, Jesus' summons in John 15 to remain in his love is "an invitation to a total belonging, to full intimacy, to an unlimited being-with" (*SJ*:165).

There is no other way to experience this depth of communion that Nouwen speaks about apart from the dynamic of prayer. Prayer and communion go together. Prayer is the expression of "[our] search for union with God" (*GD*:164). As Henri Nouwen puts it, "To pray is to move to the center of all of life and all love" (*HN*:23), entering into the depths of one's own heart where God's heart resides.

One would be hard-pressed to imagine Jesus spending an entire evening of prayer endlessly chatting his way through to his Father (Luke 6:12). Jesus must have spent large blocks of time in solitude and silence, listening to and just being with his Father and enjoying his companionship. In a way, that is what communing prayer involves—simply showing up and being present to God who is always present to us.

Thus, it can be said that true prayer involves communing with God, and true communion with God involves praying—utilizing all the various forms it takes. Communing prayer, which clearly characterized Jesus' life on earth, goes hand in hand with the combined practice of solitude, silence, and contemplation.

Solitude and silence are inseparable and together form the context within which prayer is exercised. Solitude is not merely withdrawing and being alone, but being alone with God. Silence does not mean abstaining from speaking but listening to God (WOH:69). Solitude stands for "the place of intimate encounter, the place where we commune with God" (CR:30). Thus Nouwen sensibly concludes: "the measure of [our] solitude is the measure of [our] capacity for communion" (GD:48).

Communing prayer is not only rooted in the place and practice of solitude; it also gets deepened and sustained through regular engagement with contemplation. Through contemplation we are able to catch a glimpse of God in our inner heart (CR:100). As Nouwen claims, "Contemplation is one of the surest roads to unceasing communion with the Beloved" (CR:74). Communion with God through the avenues of prayer, contemplation, silence, and solitude serves as the basis for the solid formation of a spiritual community.

Community

The combined practice of prayer, contemplation, silence, and solitude—which principally constitutes our communion experience with God—is what "grounds us in God and prepares us to live with and love others. Communion with God is where spiritual community begins."[29] Between communion and community we see a reciprocal dynamic at play: "Communion springs forth from solitude, and without a community, communion with God is impossible."[30]

Henri Nouwen believes that "solitude always calls us to community."[31] We are led to an almost mysterious sense of togetherness when solitude comes face to face with solitude and they start to greet each other. "Solitude greeting solitude" is what forms community, declares Nouwen:

Community is not the place where we are no longer alone but the place where we respect, protect, and reverently greet one another's alones. When we allow our aloneness to lead us into solitude, our solitude will enable us to rejoice in the solitude of others. (*BJ*:January 22)

Indeed, community formation forms an integral part of our spiritual life and is not optional.[32]

Commission

Henri Nouwen does not just believe that communion generates community in that "the God living in us makes us recognize the God in our fellow humans," but he is likewise convinced that community itself "always leads to mission" (*BH*:75–76). Mission, ministry, and service all serve as "the overflow of [our] love for God and for [our] fellow human beings."[33]

As Mark reminds us, Jesus called his disciples—and by extension, all of us—to be with him, to enjoy communion and intimacy with Jesus together with the rest of the spiritual community of disciples he formed so that he might commission us all into the world to share the good news (Mark 3:14).

We are all being sent on a mission just as Jesus himself was sent into the world by his Father (John 17:18). In short, we all have a mission to fulfill. Henri Nouwen remarks that "when we live our lives as missions, we become aware that there is a home from which we are sent and to which we have to return" (*BJ*:April 24). That home base may well refer to our own community. However we choose to define it and whatever else may be said about it, the fact remains that our faith community is our "spiritual home."[34] And so the dynamic cycle goes on and on.

The Cyclical Dynamic

Our missionary mandate, or commission, as the "sent" disciples of our Lord drives us back to community. For our ministry is by all means carried out within the context of community, by the community as a whole, to the community at large.[35] It is precisely the authentic experience and practice of a spiritual community that sends us back to an ever-deepening communion with our God—consequently fueling and sustaining our attempts to build community that leads to doing ministry.

Henri Nouwen insists: "You cannot *not* minister if you are in communion with God and live in community."[36] He proceeds to amplify that "the closer we come to the heart of God, the closer we come to the heart of the people of God." This deep intimacy with God's people is what then leads us to be in solidarity with the people of the world.[37] The same dynamic applies to the interconnection of solitude, community, and ministry. As Nouwen underlines it, "when you discover your belovedness by God in solitude, you see the belovedness of other people in community and can call that beauty forth in ministry."[38] For Henri Nouwen, this sequential and cyclical dynamic is so tied together that it represents a single movement of spiritual reality.

THEOLOGICAL AND SPIRITUAL DYNAMICS

Henri Nouwen's prolific influence is changing the way people view the theological and spiritual dynamics of ministry through the continuing impact of his writings. The relevance of one particular title, a small but wisdom-packed book called *In the Name of Jesus,* is captured well in a *Christianity Today* magazine quote: "*In the Name of Jesus* draws provocative and stimulating conclusions about the meaning and significance of Christian ministry."[39]

It is worth recapitulating here the message of this particular book for two specific reasons. First, it highlights the theological and spiritual dynamics of Henri Nouwen's overall concept of ministry. Second, it decidedly brings out the counterintuitive and countercultural distinctions of the principles and methods of his ministry clearly.

In the Name of Jesus is intended primarily as a book on Christian leadership but its broad principles and insights apply to ministry in general. Using images drawn from his experience with the handicapped and disabled people at L'Arche as a backdrop, Henri Nouwen weaves his entire material as a commentary on two very familiar Gospel accounts: the temptation of Jesus in the desert (Matt 4:1–11) and Peter's call to be a shepherd (John 21:15–19).

Interestingly, the three temptations of Jesus and the threefold question of Jesus to Peter complement Henri Nouwen's famous flair for structuring his material using a three-point outline. For our purposes, however, I will instead narrow it down to a dual focal point to include an expanded description of each of the temptations followed by the corresponding antidote.

The Temptation to Be Relevant

Henri Nouwen interprets Jesus' first temptation (turning stones into bread) as the perennial temptation that ministers face *to be relevant* in our success-driven and consumerist world. Whatever contexts in which we find ourselves, we are always confronted with that irresistible pull to be indispensable, competent, productive, and in control.

Author Eugene Peterson, in his prophetic book *Under the Unpredictable Plant,* confronts this all-too-familiar draw that lures many ministers who are on the verge of being "awash in...the idolatry of a religious career that they can take charge of and manage."[40] When ministers begin substituting their own sense of calling and personal vocation with the secular concept of a career, they often find themselves succumbing to the external pressure of having to deliver the ministry goods, so to speak. Somehow they have to be assured that they are worth their salt as a minister. They have to feel significant all the time, able and ready to respond to every need that is screaming to be met.

This temptation to be relevant harps on the erroneous thinking that productivity is the basis of our ministry, something that consequently distorts even our sense of identity. What makes it blinding, Nouwen warns us, is how "in a variety of ways we are made to believe that we are what we produce," thus leading us to an inordinate obsession with "products, visible results, tangible goods, and progress" (*SWC*:49–50).

Contrary to what many in our culture might expect, Henri Nouwen believes that the true minister of God is called to be "completely irrelevant and to stand in this world with nothing to offer but his or her vulnerable self" (*INJ*:17). Needless to say, this posture of humility, which incidentally Jesus modeled for us in the Gospels, is so counterculture that it does not make immediate sense. No one wishes to be marginalized; we all want to be counted and make a significant dent where we are. But Henri Nouwen insists that this kind of posturing is nowhere close to the heart of God.

The Antidote: Contemplative Prayer

What we need, Henri Nouwen declares, are ministers who know the true heart of God and are driven not by a hungry need to be significant in the world but by a desperate love for Jesus. He spells out an integrated theological and spiritual dynamic: "Knowing the heart of Jesus and loving him are the same thing" (*INJ*:27). Nouwen adds, "When we do not live in deep communion with God...then religion is easily put into the service of our desire for success, fame, and stardom" (*SJ*:164).

To minister with this kind of inner conviction, one has to be a contemplative mystic whose identity is rooted in the love of God and who practices the discipline of dwelling in God's presence through prayer (*INJ*:29). Through the regular practice of contemplative prayer, ministers learn to listen and discern God's voice and there "find the wisdom and courage to address whatever issue presents itself to them" (*INJ*:31). Most leaders in the church act and respond to needs not out of having been induced by God's prompting but by their ambition and compulsion to make something happen according to their desires and sometimes even to gain advantage.

From Henri Nouwen's perspective, prayer is as much an act of holiness as it is an act of ministry; it serves us even as it serves others. Through the discipline of prayer, we remember "that our own limited actions are rooted in the unlimited power of his name."[41] Prayer involves a humble acknowledgment of God's Creator status as opposed to our creaturely status. Therefore, for Henri Nouwen, "to pray is to walk in the full light of God, and to say simply, without holding back, 'I am human and you are God.'"[42] Ultimately, it is not our agenda that matters.

Moreover, prayer is not only an expression of our dependency upon God but also our vital interdependency with other people. In fact, "we get closest to God when we are willing to be vulnerable, when we are willing to say, 'I need somebody else.'"[43] We not only need to learn to practice the presence of God in our lives but also to practice the presence of one another in our community. It is in community "where God happens"[44]—when people pray and contemplatively listen to God and to each other in silence.

In a substantive way, Henri Nouwen's understanding of spiritual formation entails "the practicing of the paradox that prayer asks much effort but can only be received as a gift."[45] Contemplative prayer is all that; we exercise and receive it as a gift. Prayer operates as a powerful theological and spiritual dynamic to counter the creeping seduction of worldly relevance in a minister's vocation.

The Temptation to Be Spectacular

The second temptation has to do with the enticement *to be spectacular*. For Jesus, it meant having to give in to the sensational feat of throwing himself down from the pinnacle of the temple. Behind that so-called act lay an accompanying temptation to prove something. But as Nouwen says, "Jesus refused to be a stuntman" (*INJ*:38).

Our culture applauds stunts. We are forever enamored of grandiose displays of feats. As Henri Nouwen puts it, "We act as if visibility and notoriety were the main criteria of the value of what we are doing" (*SWC*:56). For many today, being spectacular is about engaging in popular, high-profile ministry activities to show off our self-sufficiency. It is tantamount to proudly parading our highly individualistic inclinations. Describing the common profile of a heroic individualist, Nouwen points to the dominant image of "the self-made man or woman who can do it all alone" (*INJ*:39).

In fact, many churches boast of their own versions of celebrity ministers because they have congregations who eagerly promote a cult-like following of their leaders. Never mind if these leaders do not have any kind of accountability whatsoever to anyone as long as everyone stands to profit from the "stardom" status that the church projects within the community.

Image has become the all-consuming passion of church life these days. "The bigger, the better" is, and has always remained, the slogan of the church. Henri Nouwen bemoans the fact that popularity has woefully replaced the true essence of ministry.

The Antidote: Confession and Forgiveness

If something needs to be inculcated constantly in the minds of ministers, it is the critical understanding that ministry is "a communal and mutual experience" (*INJ*:40). Ministry is not just done by the celebrated people in the church; ministry is everybody's undertaking—whether one is popular or not. As we minister together, "it is easier for people to recognize that we do not come in our own name, but in the name of the Lord Jesus who sent us" (*INJ*:41). In so doing it leaves no room for elevating superstars who merely end up usurping God's glory.

We would do well to also be reminded that service is not a one-way street. We minister as we ourselves are ministered to. We give as needy people who are also willing to receive in the process. The New Testament is replete with lucid passages that address the theme of mutuality in ministry within the larger context of community life. One cannot possibly ignore the numerous "one another" texts in the epistles: admonishing one another (Rom 15:7), encouraging one another (1 Thess 5:11), bearing one another's burdens (Gal 6:2), to name a few.

According to Henri Nouwen, ministers have to have the openness and humble willingness to confess their own neediness and brokenness in order to overcome the snare of what he dubs "individual heroism" (*INJ*:45). Furthermore, they need always to be ready to ask for forgiveness from the people they minister to when necessary, so that their ministry takes place within the context of a healing and reconciling presence of Jesus.

Henri Nouwen reminds us that ministers are "called to minister with their whole being, including their wounded selves" (*INJ*:50). Far from projecting a spectacular image of invincibility, we minister best out of our authentic selves—utterly powerless apart from God's infusion of power. In God's eyes, leaders and followers alike, we are all the same. We all need God desperately and we all need each other completely. In community, all of us have a vital accountability to confess and all of us have an obligation to forgive. The theological and spiritual dynamics of confession and forgiveness fill a critical role in our community since they assume "the concrete forms in which we sinful people love one another" (*INJ*:46).

The Temptation to Be Powerful

The third and final temptation is the temptation *to be powerful*. Henri Nouwen considers this to be the most seductive of all three temptations and depicts this all-pervading temptation as taking on the alarming characteristics of domination, control, and self-assertion. All these dangerous tendencies reinforce the illusion that "life is ours to dispose of" (*SWC*:61).

Indeed, there is perhaps nothing more challenging to subdue than our obsession with power. As the cliché goes, wherever we go, power is the name of the game. Nouwen reminds us of the sad reality that

> power always lusts after greater power precisely because it is an illusion. Despite our experience that power does not give us the sense of security we desire, but instead reveals our own weaknesses and limitations, we continue to make ourselves believe that more power will eventually fulfill our needs. (*SWC*:62)

As to why he perceives "the temptation of power is greatest when intimacy is a threat," Henri Nouwen offers a revealing explanation:

> Much Christian leadership is exercised by people who do not know how to develop healthy, intimate relationships and have opted for power and control instead. Many Christian empire-builders have been people unable to give and receive love. (*INJ*:60)

This is indeed so sobering but so true, as our own experiences have proven time and again.

We are reminded of the ministers who merely exercise heavy-handed authority devoid of love and concern for people. Employing high-powered control over their subordinates is often the only way they can compensate for their relational deficiency. Such leaders aggressively insist on the primacy of their position as the leader, as the one completely in charge. They reflect the hallmark traits of a culture that seems determined to infect others, even the best, in the ministry.

The Antidote: Theological Reflection

With equally determined effort, Henri Nouwen subverts such dominant forces by advocating certain countercultural incentives.

True spiritual leadership, Nouwen submits, is one in which "power is constantly abandoned in favor of love" (*INJ*:63).

Nouwen compels us to follow a different vision of maturity that Jesus espoused. This, among other things, entails having a willingness of heart to be led where we would rather not go, even if that might mean pursuing a downward path versus an upward path. As true ministers, the challenge for us is to tread the route of powerlessness, servanthood, and humility—the kind of route that our culture has serious problems validating.

As we know, Henri Nouwen walked this path himself. In his spiritual biography on Henri Nouwen, Michael O'Laughlin details some of the many decisive moves Nouwen took to stay out of the limelight:

> He immersed himself in Cistercian monasteries, Latin American slums, and Ukrainian missions. The Daybreak community, where he ultimately found a home, was a very obscure destination.[46]

The one that proved to be the greatest step downward on Nouwen's part was his choice to leave the Ivy League environment of Harvard University to live among the handicapped people at L'Arche Daybreak.

This was by no means an easy decision for Henri Nouwen. What Nouwen found extremely helpful for his own decision-making process was the same discipline he recommends for every minister to engage in habitually: the discipline of strenuous theological reflection.

Patricia O'Connell Killen and John de Beer, in their introductory book *The Art of Theological Reflection*, provide us with a helpful overview of what this particular discipline involves:

> Theological reflection is the process of seeking meaning that relies on the rich heritage of our Christian tradition as a primary source of wisdom and guidance. It presumes the profoundly incarnational (God present in our lives), providential (God caring for us), and revelatory (source of deepening knowledge of God and self) quality of human experience.[47]

The exercise of this discipline allows us to discern critically where we are being led, that is, to learn to think with the mind of Christ versus relying on our own wisdom. Doing so helps counteract the ever-present pressure for ministers to seek power other than what God provides, which, ironically is itself counterintuitive because it is the kind of power found in weakness. Theological reflection is a spiritual dynamic that ministers can never do without. We have more need of leaders and ministers who are reflective thinkers rather than activist doers, who are totally reliant upon the wisdom from above rather than upon human power and instincts.

In summary, even though many would consider relevance, popularity, and power as key ingredients of an effective ministry, they are, in reality, "not vocations but temptations" in the ministry (*INJ*:71). All three temptations lure us "to return to the ways of the world of upward mobility and divert us from our mission to reveal Christ in the world" (*SWC*:49). For Henri Nouwen, the true image of God's minister is that of a praying, vulnerable, trusting minister (*INJ*:73). It is an image that contradicts the very culture that continually presses us into a mold that even Jesus would have had trouble fitting.

Thus we have observed the dynamics of spirituality naturally and seamlessly intertwining with the dynamics of psychology, ministry, and theology. Combined, they form the launching pad that propelled Henri Nouwen's own integrated methodology for engaging the work of soul care and spiritual formation.

The integrated dynamics Henri Nouwen utilized in his ministry of formation proved to be effective not because they represented workable tools anyone could dispense on demand but because they embodied his very being—the integrated person that he was. His was a ministry of integration because his spirituality was equally one of integration.

Henri Nouwen functioned as a minister with quite a compelling sense of self-identity rooted in his realization of his true spiritual identity in Christ as God's beloved. He was able to give of himself fully to others as a friend, a guide, a mentor, and a director and managed to fulfill multiple ministry roles out of the abundance of his own experience of God's reality.

Convinced that ministry was not something he could produce on his own, Nouwen learned and lived out the priority of communing with God as the source of his service to others. With great fervor, he concretely fleshed out in his life the cyclical movement of solitude, community, and ministry without which there can be no real dynamism in our life in the Spirit.

Henri Nouwen modeled the life of a contemplative mystic who knew how to humbly see and hear God and the world. Clothed with a spirit of utter vulnerability, transparency, and authenticity, he found ready connection with people to whom he ministered, and who easily recognized his sense of realness as a person. Furthermore, Nouwen exemplified the truly sensitive and reflective individual who possesses the willingness and faith to be led by God completely in ministry.

All these are critical dynamics Henri Nouwen imbibed and integrated into his philosophy of spirituality, which consequently yielded meaningful expressions in his methodology of ministry— a ministry of integration.

Conclusion

Henri Nouwen ministered to others in a soul-deep capacity that distinguishes him as one of the most effective spiritual care providers of all time. Whether in his role as a priest, a pastor, or a prophet, Nouwen shepherded people as one who truly and deeply cared for their spiritual well-being. Whether ministering as a friend, a guide, a mentor, or a spiritual director, he did so with the clear goal of soul care and spiritual formation in mind.

Behind Henri Nouwen's deeply personal and caring focus to ministry also lies the conviction that such an approach holds relevance for our technological age: "Scientism cannot replace personalism. Techniques cannot replace ministry. Rationalism cannot replace sensitivity."[1] Given this conviction, Nouwen decried the growing tendency of "professionalization" in ministry. In his commitment to dismantle the constant elevation of hierarchy in ministry, Nouwen stressed the fact that "we are all healers who can reach out to offer health, and we all are patients in constant need of help. Only this realization can keep professionals from becoming distant technicians and those in need of care from feeling used or manipulated" (RO:93).

Ministry relationship, Henri Nouwen insisted, "can never completely be understood within the logic of a professional contract" (CM:57). Even within the field of psychotherapy itself, most therapists and counselors view the so-called therapeutic journey as an alliance, a shared task where there exists "a powerful joining of forces which energizes and supports the long, difficult and painful work of life-changing therapy." In this context, the therapist acts not as "a disinterested observer-technician, but a *fully alive human companion* for the client" (emphasis mine).[2]

In the case of Henri Nouwen, he did not just function as a "fully alive human companion"; he was, in every way, a fully alive, engaged *spiritual* companion in the journey of people's lives.

Annice Callahan condenses the creative dynamism of Henri Nouwen's philosophy and methodology of a truly spiritual ministry:

> The movement from professionalism in ministry to a spirituality of ministry is a conversion: a movement that includes both self-affirmation and self-sacrifice, a movement from a legalistic notion of contract to the biblical notion of a covenant, a movement from role-definition to careful and critical contemplation.[3]

In a life-giving way, Henri Nouwen ministered personally, spiritually, creatively, holistically, and, most of all, integratively.

In my earlier work, I noted the importance for those involved in the helping professions to learn how to be bilingually proficient in both spiritual as well as psychological language. Henri Nouwen demonstrated that kind of proficiency, but he went beyond that. In fact, he showed multilingual competency—one that takes into serious account the complex, interactive nature of humans as physical, social, psychological, and spiritual beings.

That Henri Nouwen possessed a multilingual capacity and a unique way of communicating never escaped the keen notice of his close friend, Sue Mosteller: "Henri seemed to have found a new, spiritual language that is neither theological nor psychological, utterly devoid of useless technicalities."[4] Nouwen understood that in order to be effective physicians of souls, Christian spiritual helpers—besides developing their own multilingual way of communicating—must also be conversant with the disciplines of psychology, theology, and spirituality. Indeed, the demands of soul care and spiritual formation require this type of "multitasking."[5]

Henri Nouwen did employ a multifaceted approach to spiritual formation and soul care in varying ministry situations. Without consciously structuring his philosophy and methodology, Nouwen utilized a dynamic approach that was simultaneously multilevel, multilingual, and multidisciplinary—one that smoothly combined the critical elements of practical theology, spiritual formation, psychological concepts and techniques, redemptive counseling, and pastoral care.

Little wonder, then, that Henri Nouwen's integrated and holistic approach continues to appeal irresistibly to those who embark on the ministry of spiritual formation and soul care. Without question, Nouwen's integrative style of ministry proved to be effective.

In examining Henri Nouwen's approach to the ministry of soul care and spiritual formation at close range, we can conclude that his holistic and integrative style is essentially drawn from his sophisticated understanding of the coinherence of spirituality with psychology, ministry, and theology. Henri Nouwen's ministry is characterized by a ministry of integration primarily because he, first of all, embodied a spirituality of integration. His ministry was but an overflow of his spirituality. Unquestionably, Nouwen ministered out of who he was as a person—a person of deep integrity.

I contend that Henri Nouwen's work of soul care and spiritual formation is never about techniques. Neither is it about programs and curricula—important as they are in ministry. More important, it is definitely not about "roles" even though multiple roles have been attached to his person.

In the final analysis, it is the person of Henri Nouwen that made his ministry distinct and undoubtedly fruitful. It is Nouwen's lived spirituality flowing out of his integrated being that made all the difference. Nouwen, from the start, espoused a unified schema of spirituality, consisting of three integrated movements—to self, to others, and to God (RO:13–14)—which he himself lived out. It is a spirituality of integration rooted in the Great Commandment with its equally unified and intersecting dimensions: the love of God, the love of others, and the love of self.

David Augsburger, in his book *Dissident Discipleship: A Spirituality of Self-Surrender, Love of God, and Love of Neighbor,* refers to the kind of spirituality Henri Nouwen embraced as "tripolar spirituality." There is no better way than to let the author himself articulate its essence here:

Tripolar spirituality, by definition, possesses three dimensions: it is inwardly directed, upwardly compliant, and out-

wardly committed. The spirituality of personal transformation (the inner journey), the experience of divine encounter
(the God-ward journey) and the relation of integrity and
solidarity with the neighbor (the co-human journey with
friend and enemy, with neighbor and persecutor) cannot be
divided. Tripolar spirituality sees all three as interdepen-
dent. No single one of these is fully valid apart from the
other two; no two can be extracted as primary or as actually
present without all three. I come to know myself not alone,
but in the company of fellow travelers; I come to know others not merely in collusion, but in shared commitment to the
One who brings us together justly and safely in the tri-
umphant surrender of ultimate trust. Inseparable, indivisible,
the three poles of tripolar spirituality each define and deter-
mine the authenticity of the other parts.[6]

This is the trilogy of coinherence to which Henri Nouwen
subscribed—spirituality's integral relationship with psychology,
ministry, and theology. A spirituality of integration such as this,
and which Henri Nouwen embodied, can only give way to the
ministry of integration he so effectively practiced.

Notes

PREFACE

1. See Timothy George and Alister McGrath, eds., *For All the Saints: Evangelical Theology and Christian Spirituality* (Louisville, KY: Westminster John Knox Press, 2003), 3.

INTRODUCTION

1. John Garvey, ed., *Henri Nouwen,* The Modern Spirituality Series (Springfield, IL: Templegate Publishers, 1988), 19.

2. Henri Nouwen, "My History with God," unpublished notes for the class, "Communion, Community and Ministry: An Introduction to the Spiritual Life," Regis College, Toronto (September– December 1994), 1.

3. Robert A. Jonas, ed., *Henri Nouwen: Writings Selected with an Introduction by Robert A. Jonas* (Maryknoll, NY: Orbis Books, 1998), lxi.

4. Mark R. McMinn and Todd W. Hall, introduction to *Spiritual Formation, Counseling, and Psychotherapy,* ed. Todd W. Hall and Mark R. McMinn (New York: Nova Science Publishers, 2003), ix.

5. See Robert K. Johnston, *Useless Beauty: Ecclesiastes through the Lens of Contemporary Film* (Grand Rapids: Baker, 2004), 33.

6. Charles Yrigoyen, Jr., *John Wesley: Holiness of Heart and Life* (Nashville: Abingdon Press, 1996), 22.

7. See Tony Jones, *Postmodern Youth Ministry* (Grand Rapids: Zondervan, 2001), 90.

8. Elizabeth Bounds, *Coming Together/Coming Apart: Religion, Community, and Modernity* (New York: Routledge, 1997), 27.

9. For a more elaborate discussion of this subject matter of community from Nouwen's perspective, see Wil Hernandez, *Henri*

Nouwen: A Spirituality of Imperfection (Mahwah, NJ: Paulist Press, 2006), chap. 2, 33–39.

10. Ray S. Anderson, *Spiritual Caregiving as Secular Sacrament: A Practical Theology for Professional Caregivers* (London: Jessica Kingsley Publishers, 2003), 67.

11. Jeff Imbach, "A Theology of the Heart: The Life and Writings of Henri Nouwen," Course Manual (Ministry Programs, Continuing and Distance Education Department, St. Francis Xavier University, Canada, January 2004), 1.

12. For a thorough treatment of this balance, see Hernandez, *Henri Nouwen: A Spirituality of Imperfection*, 27–44.

ONE: SPIRITUAL NURTURE OF THE SOUL

1. See Henri Nouwen, "Prayer and Health Care," *CHAC Review* 17 (Winter 1989): 11–16.

2. For an excellent "genealogical" summary of the history, sources, and meaning of the terms *nephesh, psyche, anima,* and *soul* in the West, see Eric L. Johnson, "Whatever Happened to the Human Soul? A Brief Christian Genealogy of a Psychological Term," *Journal of Psychology and Theology* 26 (Spring 1998): 16–28.

3. Wayne G. Rollins, *Soul and Psyche: The Bible in Psychological Perspective* (Minneapolis: Fortress Press, 1999), 4–6.

4. David Fontana, *Psychology, Religion, and Spirituality* (Oxford, UK: Blackwell, 2003), 25.

5. Rollins, *Soul and Psyche*, 6.

6. Ibid., 95.

7. Cf. *New Illustrated Bible Dictionary* (Nashville: Thomas Nelson, 1995), 1195–96. See Mark 8:34–37, where "soul" is used synonymously with "life." See also Matt 26:38 and Luke 1:46, where the word *soul* seems to point to one's inner self or personality.

8. Ray S. Anderson, *The New Age of Soul: Spiritual Wisdom for a New Millennium* (Eugene, OR: Wipf & Stock, 2001), 39.

9. Ronald Rolheiser, *The Holy Longing: The Search for a Christian Spirituality* (New York: Doubleday, 1999), 12–13.

10. Robert L. Wise, *Quest for the Soul* (Nashville: Thomas Nelson, 1996), 90.

11. Gerald G. May, *Addiction and Grace: Love and Spirituality in the Healing of Addictions* (New York: HarperCollins, 1991), 64.

12. Cf. Karl Barth, *Church Dogmatics,* vol. III, pt. 2 (Edinburgh: T. & T. Clark, 1960), 327.

13. James R. Beck, "Self and Soul: Exploring the Boundary

Between Psychotherapy and Spiritual Direction," *Journal of Psychology and Theology* 31 (Spring 2003): 28.

14. May, *Addiction and Grace,* n. 1 (chap. 4), 186.

15. Gerald G. May, *The Dark Night of the Soul: A Psychiatrist Explores the Connection Between Darkness and Spiritual Growth* (San Francisco: HarperSanFrancisco, 2004), 42.

16. Shirley Darcus Sullivan, *Transformed by Love* (New York: New City Press, 2002), 12.

17. See Charles Gerkin, *The Living Human Document: Revisioning Pastoral Counseling in a Hermeneutical Mode* (Nashville: Abingdon Press, 1984), 98.

18. See Robert Watson, "Toward Union in Love: The Contemplative Spiritual Tradition and Contemporary Psychoanalytic Theory in the Formation of Persons," in *Spiritual Formation, Counseling, and Psychotherapy,* ed. Todd W. Hall and Mark R. McMinn (New York: Nova Science Publishers, 2003), 57.

19. I owe this specific insight to Dr. David Augsburger, who points out that in biblical thought, soul has the given sense of being "graced."

20. David G. Benner, *Sacred Companions: The Gift of Spiritual Friendship and Direction* (Downers Grove: InterVarsity, 2002), 37.

21. Sue Monk Kidd, *When the Heart Waits: Spiritual Direction for Life's Sacred Questions* (San Francisco: HarperSanFrancisco, 1990), 52–53.

22. See John T. McNeill, *A History of the Cure of Souls* (New York: Harper & Brothers, 1951).

23. See Eugene H. Peterson, *The Contemplative Pastor: Returning to the Art of Spiritual Direction* (Grand Rapids: Eerdmans, 1993), 57.

24. David G. Benner, *Care of Souls: Revisioning Christian Nurture and Counsel* (Grand Rapids: Baker, 1998), 28, 21, 32.

25. Thomas Oden, *Pastoral Theology: Essentials of Ministry* (San Francisco: Harper & Row, 1983), 187.

26. Jay M. Uomoto, "Human Suffering, Psychotherapy and Soul Care: The Spirituality of Henri Nouwen at the Nexus," *Journal of Psychology and Christianity* 14 (Winter 1995): 347, 352.

27. Ray S. Anderson, *Spiritual Caregiving as Secular Sacrament: A Practical Theology for Professional Caregivers* (London: Jessica Kingsley Publishers, 2003), 15.

28. Carl G. Jung, *Modern Man in Search of a Soul* (New York: Harcourt Brace, 1939), 262.

29. See Charles F. Kemp, *Physicians of the Soul* (New York: The Macmillan Company, 1947), 226–42.

30. Tilden Edwards, *Spiritual Friend: Reclaiming the Gift of Spiritual Direction* (New York: Paulist Press, 1980), 125.

31. See Seward Hiltner, *Preface to Pastoral Theology* (New York: Abingdon Press, 1954), pt. III passim; 69.

32. Sue Mosteller, interview by the author, tape recording, Richmond Hill, Ontario, April 26, 2004.

33. Robert Durback, *Seeds of Hope: A Henri Nouwen Reader* (New York: Bantam Books, 1989), xxii.

34. Michael Ford, "My Search for Henri," in *Befriending Life: Encounters with Henri Nouwen*, ed. Beth Porter with Susan M. S. Brown and Philip Coulter (New York: Doubleday, 2001), 210.

35. Mary Bastedo, "Henri and Daybreak: A Story of Mutual Transformation," in *Befriending Life,* 33.

36. Nathan Ball, interview by the author, tape recording, Richmond Hill, Ontario, April 27, 2004. Also based on an informal lunch conversation with the author, Richmond Hill, Ontario, April 28, 2004.

37. Gerald S. Twomey and Claude Pomerlau, eds., *Remembering Henri* (Maryknoll, NY: Orbis Books, 2006), 130.

38. Annice Callahan, *Spiritual Guides for Today* (New York: Crossroad, 1992), 118–34.

39. Charles R. Ringma, *The Seeking Heart: A Journey with Henri Nouwen* (Brewster, MA: Paraclete Press, 2006), xvii–xviii.

40. See Bruce Demarest, *Satisfy Your Soul: Restoring the Heart of Christian Spirituality* (Colorado Springs: NavPress, 1999), 190–218. Cf. idem, *Soul Guide: Following Jesus As Spiritual Director* (Colorado Springs: NavPress, 2003), 36–43.

41. Henri Nouwen, introduction to *Soul Friend: The Practice of Christian Spirituality,* by Kenneth Leech (New York: Harper & Row, 1980), viii.

42. See Tilden Edwards, *Spiritual Director, Spiritual Companion: Guide to Tending the Soul* (Mahwah, NJ: Paulist Press, 2001), 97–102.

43. See Demarest, *Satisfy Your Soul,* 191–95, and *Soul Guide,* 37–40.

TWO: SPIRITUAL COMPANION—FRIEND AND GUIDE

1. David G. Benner, *Sacred Companions: The Gift of Spiritual Friendship and Direction* (Downers Grove: InterVarsity, 2002), 77.

2. See Sue Mosteller, foreword to *Sabbatical Journey: The Diary of His Final Year*, by Henri Nouwen (New York: Crossroad, 1998), vii. Cf. Michael O'Laughlin, *God's Beloved: A Spiritual Biography of Henri Nouwen* (Maryknoll, NY: Orbis Books, 2004), 6–7.

3. Aelred of Rievaulx, *Spiritual Friendship,* trans. Mary Eugenia Laker and intro. Douglass Roby (Kalamazoo, MI: Cistercian Publications, 1974), 23.

4. Benner, *Sacred Companions,* 84.

5. Richard J. Woods, *The Spirituality of the Celtic Saints* (Maryknoll, NY: Orbis Books, 2000), 62.

6. Charles R. Ringma, *The Seeking Heart: A Journey with Henri Nouwen* (Brewster, MA: Paraclete Press, 2006), 79.

7. Jean Vanier, "A Gentle Instrument of a Loving God," in *Befriending Life: Encounters with Henri Nouwen,* ed. Beth Porter with Susan M. S. Brown and Philip Coulter (New York: Doubleday, 2001), 261.

8. This and the following five paragraphs contain paraphrased accounts that are based upon the interview with Mosteller by the author, April 26, 2004.

9. Michael O'Laughlin, *Henri Nouwen: His Life and Vision* (Maryknoll, NY: Orbis Books, 2005), 128.

10. Nathan Ball, "A Covenant of Friendship," in *Befriending Life,* 92. Unless otherwise noted, subsequent references to Ball's relationship with Nouwen are quoted from this source.

11. Aelred of Rievaulx, *Spiritual Friendship,* 61.

12. O'Laughlin, *Henri Nouwen: His Life and Vision,* 129.

13. This account is based on the interview by the author, April 27, 2004.

14. Ringma, *The Seeking Heart,* 94–95.

15. Jeff Imbach, introduction to *Words of Hope and Healing: 99 Sayings by Henri Nouwen* (New York: New City Press, 2005), n.p.

16. See Henri Nouwen's personal account of this dark episode in his life in *The Inner Voice of Love: A Journey Through Anguish to Freedom* (New York: Image Books, 1996), xiii–xix.

17. John Catoir, "Journey's End, Journey's Beginning," in *Nouwen Then: Personal Reflections on Henri,* ed. Christopher de Vinck (Grand Rapids: Zondervan, 1999), 134.

18. O'Laughlin, *Henri Nouwen: His Life and Vision,* 132.

19. Mindy Caliguire, *Spiritual Friendship* (Downers Grove: IVP Connect, 2007), 72.

20. Chris Glaser, "Henri's Legacy," in *Remembering Henri,* ed.

Gerald S. Twomey and Claude Pomerlau (Maryknoll, NY: Orbis Books, 2006), 142.

21. Carolyn Gratton, *The Art of Spiritual Guidance* (New York: Crossroad, 1992), 165.

22. See, e.g., Thomas Merton, *Spiritual Direction and Meditation* (Collegeville, MN: The Liturgical Press, 1960); W. Paul Jones, *The Art of Spiritual Direction: Giving and Receiving Spiritual Guidance* (Nashville: Upper Room Books, 2002); Gerald G. May, *Care of Mind, Care of Spirit: A Psychiatrist Explores Spiritual Direction* (New York: HarperCollins, 1992).

23. Howard Rice, *The Pastor as Spiritual Guide* (Nashville: Upper Room Books, 1998), 62, 91–139.

24. Morton T. Kelsey, *Companions on the Inner Way: The Art of Spiritual Guidance* (New York: Crossroad, 1983), 7.

25. Marjorie J. Thompson, *Soul Feast: An Invitation to the Christian Spiritual Life* (Louisville, KY: Westminster John Knox Press, 1995), 103.

26. Henri J. M. Nouwen, *The Dance of Life: Weaving Sorrows and Blessings into One Joyful Step,* ed. Michael Ford (Notre Dame, IN: Ave Maria Press, 2005), 34.

27. Henri Nouwen with Michael J. Christensen and Rebecca J. Laird, *Spiritual Direction: Wisdom for the Long Walk of Faith* (San Francisco: HarperSanFrancisco, 2006), 9.

28. Kelsey, *Companions on the Inner Way,* 59.

29. Nouwen, *The Dance of Life,* 34.

30. Deirdre LaNoue, *The Spiritual Legacy of Henri Nouwen* (New York: Continuum, 2000), 138.

31. Vanier, "A Gentle Instrument of a Loving God," 261.

32. Art Laffin, "Faith, Friendship, Peacemaking," in *Befriending Life,* 229; also 224.

33. Jack Stroh, "A Map for Life," in *Befriending Life,* 204.

34. Based on the phone interview by the author, August 10, 2007.

35. Andrew Dreitcer, phone interview by the author, July 30, 2007.

36. Alan Steers and Judy Steers, "Sowing in Tears, Reaping in Joy," in *Befriending Life,* 216.

37. Thompson, *Soul Feast,* 104.

38. Based upon the author's phone interview with Lisa Cataldo, August 9, 2007.

39. Annice Callahan, "Henri Nouwen: The Heart as Home," in *Spiritualities of the Heart: Approaches to Personal Wholeness in Christian Tradition,* ed. Annice Callahan (Mahwah, NJ: Paulist Press, 1990), 212.

40. Henri Nouwen, *The Only Necessary Thing: Living a Prayerful Life,* comp. and ed. Wendy Wilson Greer (New York: Crossroad, 1999), 19.

THREE: SPIRITUAL COMPANION— MENTOR AND DIRECTOR

1. Bruce Demarest, *Soul Guide: Following Jesus as Spiritual Director* (Colorado Springs: NavPress, 2003), 37.

2. Ibid. See Bobb Biehl, *Mentoring: Confidence in Finding a Mentor and Becoming One* (Nashville: Broadman & Holman, 1996), 30.

3. Ibid., 50. *Mentoree* is the authors' preferred term over the more technical designation mentee (36).

4. James M. Houston, foreword to *Spiritual Mentoring: A Guide for Seeking and Giving Direction* by Keith R. Anderson and Randy D. Reese (Downers Grove: InterVarsity, 1999), 9.

5. This account is based on the interview with Joe Vorstermans by the author, tape recording, Richmond Hill, Ontario, April 28, 2004.

6. Joe Vorstermans, "Hands of Love," in *Befriending Life: Encounters with Henri Nouwen,* ed. Beth Porter with Susan M. S. Brown and Philip Coulter (New York: Doubleday, 2001), 255.

7. Based on the phone interview with Vorstermans by the author, August 10, 2007.

8. Based on the taped interview with Vorstermans by the author, April 28, 2004, and follow-up phone interview, August 10, 2007.

9. Based on the phone interview with Vorstermans by the author, August 10, 2007.

10. Andrew Kennedy, "A New Way to Live," in *Befriending Life,* 40ff.; 40–41.

11. Kathy Christie, "Working with Henri," in *Befriending Life,* 137.

12. Siobhan Keogh, phone interview with the author, August 27, 2007.

13. Beth Porter, "Lessons in Openness," in *Befriending Life,* 189.

14. Wendy Lywood, "Rediscovering My Priesthood," in *Befriending Life,* 232.

15. Based on the taped interview with Wendy Lywood by the author, tape recording, Richmond Hill, Ontario, April 29, 2004.

16. Lywood, "Rediscovering My Priesthood," 237.

17. See Anderson and Reese, *Spiritual Mentoring,* 13, 59. Cf. J. Robert Clinton and Richard W. Clinton, *The Mentor Handbook:*

Detailed Guidelines and Helps for Christian Mentors and Mentorees (Altadena, CA: Barnabas Publishers, 1991).

18. The next five paragraphs are based on the phone interview with Lywood by the author, August 27, 2007.

19. Demarest, *Soul Guide*, 37.

20. Anderson and Reese, *Spiritual Mentoring*, 155.

21. Keogh, phone interview with the author, August 27, 2007.

22. Parker J. Palmer, *Let Your Life Speak: Listening for the Voice of Vocation* (San Francisco: Jossey-Bass, 2000), 57.

23. Ronald Rolheiser, *The Holy Longing: The Search for a Christian Spirituality* (New York: Doubleday, 1999), v.

24. See Janet K. Ruffing, *Spiritual Direction: Beyond the Beginnings* (Mahwah, NJ: Paulist Press, 2000), 1.

25. Alan Jones, *Exploring Spiritual Direction*, new ed. (Boston, MA: Cowley Publications, 1999), 154.

26. Gary W. Moon and David G. Benner, afterword to *Spiritual Direction and the Care of Souls: A Guide to Christian Approaches and Practices*, ed. Gary W. Moon and David G. Benner (Downers Grove: InterVarsity, 2004), 245.

27. Henri Nouwen, "Spiritual Direction," *Worship* 55 (September 1981): 399.

28. Henri Nouwen with Michael J. Christensen and Rebecca J. Laird, *Spiritual Direction: Wisdom for the Long Walk of Faith* (San Francisco: HarperSanFrancisco, 2006), ix.

29. Nouwen, "Spiritual Direction," 402.

30. Henri Nouwen, introduction to *Soul Friend: An Invitation to Spiritual Direction*, by Kenneth Leech (New York: HarperCollins, 1980), ix.

31. Lorenzo Sforza-Cesarini, "The Necessity of Prayer," in *Befriending Life*, 251.

32. Henri Nouwen, foreword to *Spiritual Direction: An Invitation to Abundant Life*, by Francis Vanderwall (New York: Paulist Press, 1981), x, vi.

33. Nouwen with Christensen and Laird, *Spiritual Direction*, 62.

34. Ibid., 61.

35. Ibid., 62.

36. Ibid., 63.

37. Nouwen, foreword to *Spiritual Direction*, x.

38. Damien Isabell, foreword to *From Resentment to Gratitude*, by Henri Nouwen (Chicago: Franciscan Herald Press, 1974), 9.

39. Susan Zimmerman, "Just Henri," in *Befriending Life*, 142–43.

40. Cataldo, "The Reality Principle," in *Befriending Life*, 64, 66.

41. Cataldo, phone conversation with the author, October 2, 2004.

42. Nouwen with Christensen and Laird, *Spiritual Direction*, 22.

43. See Nouwen, foreword to *Spiritual Direction*, x.

44. Keogh, "My Adopted Father," in *Befriending Life*, 161.

45. Keogh, electronic mail correspondence with the author, October 4, 2004.

46. Cataldo, phone conversation with the author, August 9, 2007.

47. Sforza-Cesarini, "The Necessity of Prayer," 250.

48. Based on the phone interview with the author, July 30, 2007.

49. Andrew Dreitcer, "Traveling Without a Map," in *Nouwen Then*, 87.

FOUR: A MINISTRY OF INTEGRATION

1. See Michael J. Christensen, "Henri as Spiritual Guide," in *Remembering Henri*, ed. Gerald S. Twomey and Claude Pomerlau (Maryknoll, NY: Orbis Books, 2006), 38–44.

2. Henri Nouwen, "Contemplation and Action," a sermon preached at St. Paul's Church, Columbia University, December 10, 1978 (The Henri J. M. Nouwen Archives and Research Collection, John M. Kelly Library, University of St. Michael's College, Toronto), 3.

3. Gary W. Moon, "Two Trees–Two Selves," *Conversations: A Forum for Authentic Transformation* (Fall 2003): 46.

4. C. S. Lewis, *Mere Christianity* (New York: The Macmillan Company, 1964), 175.

5. David G. Benner, *The Gift of Being Yourself: The Sacred Call to Self-Discovery* (Downers Grove: InterVarsity, 2004), 91.

6. R. D. Laing, *The Divided Self* (New York: Pantheon Books, 1960), 100.

7. See M. Basil Pennington, *True Self/False Self: Unmasking the Spirit Within* (New York: Crossroad, 2000), chap. 2.

8. Kenneth Boa, "Forming an Authentic Self in an Inauthentic World," *Conversations* (Fall 2003): 32.

9. M. Robert Mulholland, Jr., *The Deeper Journey: The Spirituality of Discovering Your True Self* (Downers Grove: InterVarsity, 2006), 42.

10. Ibid., 30–42.

11. Ellen T. Charry, "Theology After Psychology," in *Care for the Soul: Exploring the Intersection of Psychology and Theology*, ed.

Mark R. McMinn and Timothy Phillips (Downers Grove: Inter-Varsity, 2001), 126.

12. James Finley, *Merton's Palace of Nowhere*, 25th anniversary ed. (Notre Dame: Ave Maria Press, 2003), 21.

13. One important side note to keep in mind is that our new identity in Christ (i.e., our new self) is not to be equated with the *imago dei,* which has been marred by the fall but which is gradually being restored to its original condition via the redemptive power of our new self in Christ (see Boa, "Forming an Authentic Self," 32–33).

14. See Byung-Mo Yang, "A Study of Pastoral Identity in Light of the Works of Henri J. M. Nouwen and Its Implications for the Korean Pastoral Context" (PhD diss., Southwestern Baptist Theological Seminary, 2002), 10–11.

15. Henri Nouwen, "Living in the Center Enables Us to Care," *Health Progress* 71 (July–August 1990): 53.

16. Michael O'Laughlin, *God's Beloved: A Spiritual Biography of Henri Nouwen* (Maryknoll, NY: Orbis Books, 2004), 162.

17. Jeffrey Allan Kisner, "Self-Disclosing Stories in Sermons: A Multidisciplinary Rationale" (PhD diss., The Southern Baptist Theological Seminary, 1989), 115.

18. Alastair V. Campbell, *Rediscovering Pastoral Care* (London: Darton, Longman and Todd, 1981), 101.

19. See Kisner, "Self-Disclosing Stories," 116.

20. Henri Nouwen and Walter J. Gaffney, *Aging: The Fulfillment of Life* (New York: Image Books, 1990), 95.

21. See Kisner, "Self-Disclosing Stories."

22. Stephen Kendrick, "In Touch with the Blessing: An Interview with Henri Nouwen," *Christian Century* (March 1993): 320.

23. Marci Whitney-Schenck, "The Wounded Healer," *Christianity and the Arts* (Spring 1999): 8.

24. Nouwen and Gaffney, *Aging,* 97.

25. Ibid., 117.

26. Bob Massie, "God's Restless Servant," in *Befriending Life: Encounters with Henri Nouwen,* ed. Beth Porter with Susan M. S. Brown and Philip Coulter (New York: Doubleday, 2001), 7.

27. See Henri Nouwen, "Moving from Solitude to Community and Ministry," *Leadership* (Spring 1995): 81.

28. Henri Nouwen with Michael J. Christensen and Rebecca J. Laird, *Spiritual Direction: Wisdom for the Long Walk of Faith* (San Francisco: HarperSanFrancisco, 2006), 110.

29. Ibid., 112.

30. Ibid., 115.

31. Ibid., 112.

32. Ibid., 115.

33. Rebecca Laird, "Parting Words: A Conversation with Henri Nouwen," *Sacred Journey: The Journal of Fellowship in Prayer* 47 (December 1996): 13.

34. See Nouwen with Christensen and Laird, *Spiritual Direction,* 113.

35. For an expanded treatment of this thought, see Wil Hernandez, *Henri Nouwen: A Spirituality of Imperfection* (Mahwah, NJ: Paulist Press, 2006), 33–37.

36. Arthur Boers, "What Henri Nouwen Found at Daybreak: Experiments in Spiritual Living in a Secular World," *Christianity Today* 38 (October 3, 1994): 28.

37. Henri Nouwen, "Intimacy, Fecundity and Ecstasy," *Radix* n.v. (May–June, 1984): 10.

38. Nouwen with Christensen and Laird, *Spiritual Direction,* 125.

39. Quoted on the back cover of the book *In the Name of Jesus.*

40. Eugene H. Peterson, *Under the Unpredictable Plant: An Exploration in Vocational Holiness* (Grand Rapids: Eerdmans, 1992), 4.

41. Henri Nouwen, *Prayer and the Priest* (Chicago: Franciscan Herald Press, 1980), 19; see also 13.

42. Henri Nouwen, "Confessing Helplessness," in *The Contemporaries Meet the Classics in Prayer,* comp. Leonard Allen (West Monroe, LA: Howard Publishing, 2003), 186.

43. Quoted in Robert Barron and Donald Senior, *Opening Hearts, Minds and Doors: Embodying the Inclusive and Vulnerable Love of God* (Chicago: National Federation of Priests' Councils, 1999), 9.

44. I am lifting this phrase from Archbishop of Canterbury Rowan William's book of the same title (see *Where God Happens: Discovering Christ in One Another* [Boston: New Seeds Books, 2005]).

45. Henri Nouwen, *From Resentment to Gratitude* (Chicago: Franciscan Herald Press, 1974), 30.

46. O'Laughlin, *God's Beloved,* 60–61.

47. Patricia O'Connell Killen and John de Beer, *The Art of Theological Reflection* (New York: Crossroad, 1994), xi.

CONCLUSION

1. Charles Ringma, *Dare to Journey with Henri Nouwen* (Metro Manila, Philippines: OMF Literature, 1995), app. I, unpaginated.

2. James F. T. Bugental, *The Art of the Psychotherapist* (New York: Norton, 1987), 49.

3. Annice Callahan, *Spiritual Guides for Today* (New York: Crossroad, 1992), 126. Cf. Nouwen, *Creative Ministry*, 41–65.

4. Sue Mosteller, interview by the author, tape recording, Richmond Hill, Ontario, April 26, 2004.

5. Mark R. McMinn, *Psychology, Theology, and Spirituality in Christian Counseling* (Wheaton, IL: Tyndale House, 1996), 270.

6. David Augsburger, *Dissident Discipleship: A Spirituality of Self-Surrender, Love of God, and Love of Neighbor* (Grand Rapids: Brazos Press, 2006), 13.

Selected Bibliography

Primary Sources on Henri J. M. Nouwen

Beyond the Mirror: Reflections on Death and Life. New York: Crossroad, 2001.

Bread for the Journey: A Daybook of Wisdom and Faith. San Francisco: HarperSanFrancisco, 1997.

Can You Drink the Cup? Notre Dame: Ave Maria Press, 1996.

Clowning in Rome: Reflections on Solitude, Celibacy, Prayer, and Contemplation. New York: Image Books, 2000.

Creative Ministry. New York: Image Books, 1978.

A Cry for Mercy: Prayers from the Genesee. New York: Image Books, 1981.

Encounters with Merton: Spiritual Reflections. 2d ed. New York: Crossroad, 1972, 1981.

The Genesee Diary: Report from a Trappist Monastery. New York: Image Books, 1989.

¡Gracias! A Latin American Journal. Maryknoll, NY: Orbis Books, 1993.

Here and Now: Living in the Spirit. New York: Crossroad, 1994.

In the Name of Jesus: Reflections on Christian Leadership. New York: Crossroad, 1989.

The Inner Voice of Love: A Journey Through Anguish to Freedom. New York: Image Books, 1996.

Lifesigns: Intimacy, Fecundity, and Ecstasy in Christian Perspective. New York: Doubleday, 1986.

The Living Reminder: Service and Prayer in Memory of Jesus Christ. San Francisco: HarperSanFrancisco, 1977.

Our Greatest Gift: A Meditation on Death and Dying. New York: HarperCollins, 1995.

Reaching Out: The Three Movements of the Spiritual Life. New York: Doubleday, 1975.

The Return of the Prodigal Son: A Story of Homecoming. New York: Image Books, 1994.

The Road to Daybreak: A Spiritual Journey. New York: Doubleday, 1988.

Sabbatical Journey. New York: Crossroad, 1998.

The Selfless Way of Christ: Downward Mobility and the Spiritual Life. Maryknoll, NY: Orbis Books, 2007.

Show Me the Way: Readings for Each Day of Lent. New York: Crossroad, 1992.

The Way of the Heart: Desert Spirituality and Contemporary Ministry. New York: HarperCollins, 1991.

With Burning Hearts: A Meditation on the Eucharistic Life. Maryknoll, NY: Orbis Books, 1994.

The Wounded Healer: Ministry in Contemporary Society. New York: Image Books, 1979.

Index

About the Author

WIL HERNANDEZ was born and raised in the Philippines. Prior to coming to the United States in 1995 to pursue his master of theology degree, he worked full-time with an international, interdenominational parachurch organization for eighteen years. Wil finished his PhD in practical theology with a concentration in spirituality / spiritual formation in 2005 at Fuller Theological Seminary. Currently, he works for the Leadership Institute (www.tli.cc) in partnership with the Denver-based Spiritual Formation Alliance Network. He serves as the coordinator of the Southern California Spiritual Formation Partners and also teaches courses in spirituality at various seminaries and universities, including Fuller Seminary, Azusa Pacific University, and Loyola Marymount University.

A trained counselor and spiritual director, Wil devotes a big part of his time "companioning" others in their spiritual journey. All year round, he conducts retreats, classes, workshops, seminars, and lectures, focusing on the spirituality of Henri Nouwen. He is the author of *Henri Nouwen: A Spirituality of Imperfection,* published by Paulist Press in 2006.

Wil has been married to Juliet for nearly twenty-four years, and together with their two sons, Jonathan and David, they make their home in Arcadia, California.

For more information
about the Henri Nouwen courses,
retreats, seminars, and workshops
that Wil Hernandez regularly conducts,
please visit

www. nouwenlegacy.com

or e-mail Wil at

wil@nouwenlegacy.com